Advanced Introduction to Antitheodicy

Advanced Introduction to Antitheodicy

Sami Pihlström
University of Helsinki, Finland
sami.pihlstrom@helsinki.fi

ANTHEM PRESS

Anthem Press
An imprint of Wimbledon Publishing Company
www.anthempress.com

This edition first published in UK and USA 2026
by ANTHEM PRESS
75–76 Blackfriars Road, London SE1 8HA, UK
or PO Box 9779, London SW19 7ZG, UK
and
244 Madison Ave #116, New York, NY 10016, USA

Copyright © 2026 Sami Pihlström

The author asserts the moral right to be identified as the author of this work.

All rights reserved. Without limiting the rights under copyright reserved above,
no part of this publication may be reproduced, stored or introduced into
a retrieval system, or transmitted, in any form or by any means
(electronic, mechanical, photocopying, recording or otherwise),
without the prior written permission of both the copyright
owner and the above publisher of this book.

British Library Cataloguing-in-Publication Data
A catalogue record for this book is available from the British Library.

Library of Congress Cataloging-in-Publication Data: 2025949373
A catalog record for this book has been requested.

ISBN-13 (HB): 978-1-83999-677-1
ISBN-10 (HB): 1-83999-677-3

ISBN-13 (PB): 978-1-83999-678-8
ISBN-10 (PB): 1-83999-678-1

This title is also available as an eBook.

CONTENTS

Acknowledgments		vii
1.	Introduction	1
2.	Conceptual and Methodological Preliminaries	13
3.	A Sketch of the History of Antitheodicy	31
4.	Secular Theodicies and Contemporary Antitheodicism	59
5.	Antitheodicy and Ethical Seriousness	77
6.	Conclusion	115
References		123
Index		131

ACKNOWLEDGMENTS

I have examined the problem of evil and suffering – and defended an antitheodicist approach to it – in relation to a range of issues in ethics, metaphysics, and the philosophy of religion, since the early years of this century. While the views developed in this book are, inevitably, somewhat indebted to my extensive earlier research on the topic (e.g., Pihlström 2013, 2014, 2017, 2019, 2020a, 2020b, 2021, 2023, 2025; Kivistö and Pihlström 2016, 2017; Pihlström and Kivistö 2023), the present volume is a novel and self-standing attempt to introduce antitheodicy and to argue for its philosophical and ethical significance. I will utilize many of the ideas, arguments, references, and literature reviews that are available, in a considerably more comprehensive form, in my earlier publications on these issues, but I will not directly repeat those earlier discussions here. The only previously written paper of mine that is partially used here (in a heavily revised and rewritten form) is "Secular Theodicies: A Transcendental-Pragmatist Critique," forthcoming (2026) in a collection of essays on theodicy and antitheodicy edited by Francis Jonbäck and Lauri Snellman.

In particular, I must in this volume set aside the literary explorations of theodicies and antitheodicies that play a central role in my joint work with Sari Kivistö. My approach in this introduction is rather purely philosophical, but this of course does not entail that I would not find literary articulations of the philosophical problems to be discussed of utmost relevance to our understanding of evil, suffering, ethics, and the human condition. In our joint investigations of antitheodicism (Kivistö and Pihlström 2016, 2017; Pihlström and Kivistö 2023), we analyze a wide selection of literary works, including the biblical *Book of Job*, Dostoevsky's *The Brothers Karamazov* (an unavoidable reference in all antitheodicy reflections, including this book), Kafka's *The Trial*, Beckett's *Waiting for Godot*, Orwell's *Nineteen Eighty-Four*, Camus's *The Plague*, Joseph Roth's *Hiob*, and Philip Roth's *Nemesis*. Here I must, unfortunately, mostly bracket such literary references (apart from a few inescapable ones to Dostoevsky and Camus), but I encourage my literary-minded readers to find distinctive expressions of philosophical themes such as antitheodicy in these and many other works. Almost all serious literature deals with suffering in one way or another.

Over the years, at least since the early 2010s, I have given dozens of talks and conference papers on antitheodicy and antitheodicism in many different countries and in a variety of academic contexts. It would be impossible to specifically acknowledge all those who have made a difference to how my ideas and arguments have developed. However, I should like to thank a number of friends and colleagues whose comments have significantly, over the years and even decades, contributed to my understanding of evil, suffering, and antitheodicy, as well as ethics and philosophy of religion generally, in specific ways that are at least implicit (and in some cases explicit) in this book. These individuals include, among many others, Dirk-Martin Grube, Lars Hertzberg, Ana Honnacker, Francis Jonbäck, the late Simo Knuuttila, Timo Koistinen, Virpi Mäkinen, Ilkka Niiniluoto, Wayne Proudfoot, Panu-Matti Pöykkö, Alex Rakhmanin, Henrik Rydenfelt, Risto Saarinen, Naoko Saito, Lauri Snellman, Paul Standish, Nick Trakakis, Tommi Uschanov, Terhi Utriainen, Oliver Wiertz, and Ulf Zackariasson – as well as the numerous students who have attended my classes on suffering, evil, death, and related topics at the University of Helsinki since 2016.

This book is part of my publishing activities within my research project on secular theodicies and their pragmatist critique, funded by the Research Council of Finland and hosted by the Faculty of Theology, University of Helsinki (2024–2028), as well as one of the first results of my new major project, the Centre of Excellence "Meliorist Philosophy of Suffering," also funded by the Research Council of Finland (2026–2033). I should like to thank Jebaslin Hephzibah and Gomathy Ilammathe at Anthem Press, as well as an anonymous reviewer for helpful constructive criticism. Needless to say, any errors and misunderstandings that may remain are exclusively mine.

Most importantly, I am obviously deeply indebted to Sari Kivistö as well as my daughters, Meeri and Katri, not only for continuous discussions on many of the topics of this book but for the spirit of seriousness that makes those issues urgent – and for everything else, for that matter.

Helsinki, November 2025
Sami Pihlström

Chapter 1
INTRODUCTION

We all know that the world we live in, though containing pleasurable and meaningful moments, is also a world of pain and suffering – at the individual level of our private lives as well as the more general level of historical and political events. The familiar examples of suffering we encounter and ethically need to engage with range from everyday cases of unpleasantness, such as a prolonged illness or financial trouble, to massive horrors epitomized in world wars and genocides, such as, at the extreme, the Holocaust. Furthermore, we know, in most cases, how to *explain* these evils: medical science tells us how and why various illnesses occur, geology explains earthquakes, and history and social psychology may explain what happened at the darkest hours of our civilization, and why. However, even when everything has been explained, many of us feel that we still fail to properly understand why unspeakable events like brutal mass murders and crimes against humanity have taken place. Especially those of us with religious convictions may wonder why God, if God exists, allows such things to exist. The theological and philosophical tradition of *theodicy* is an influential attempt to respond to such questions that focus not so much on (everyday or scientific) explanations of suffering but on the normative question of *justifying* or *excusing* the reality of suffering. Theodicies attempt to philosophically or theologically explain why sufferings may have a useful function, play a purposive role, serve "good" intentions, or be unavoidable side effects of something that is in itself beneficial – if not to the suffering individual, then at least to humankind (or the world) at large.

This book introduces the concept of *antitheodicy* and an approach I propose to call *antitheodicism* as central elements of a critical ethical response to the need to engage with the reality of evil and suffering. In particular, antitheodicy is, of course, a critical response to the theodicy tradition. While the mainstream debate on the problem of evil and suffering in the philosophy of religion continues to focus on theodicies and "defenses" seeking to justify or excuse God's allowing that there is apparently meaningless suffering (which, then, ceases to be meaningless when we understand God's reasons, or at least possible reasons, for allowing this), the present introduction not only seeks to show why an antitheodicist alternative is ethically superior to such attempts but also, arguably even more importantly, extends the antitheodicist approach from the narrow confines of philosophy of religion to broader ethical engagements with suffering.

Clearly, there is no antitheodicy without theodicy. Therefore, introducing antitheodicy and antitheodicism is subordinate to the theodicy discourse, which again presupposes the entire history of the problem of evil and suffering, particularly the so-called argument from evil to which theodicies are typically put forward as responses. However, this inquiry focuses on antitheodicy: no detailed discussion of different theodicies can be provided; rather, the assumption that a theodicy ought to be formulated in the first place will be challenged at a meta-level. For extensive accounts of the problem of evil and suffering in general and its theological and philosophical history, as well as the various theodicies proposed as alleged solutions to the problem, the reader is referred to a range of introductory works in the philosophy of religion, as well as many collections of articles addressing the problem of evil.[1] Here the central ideas of theodicy and theodicism are explained only to the extent that the antitheodicist criticism of theodicies – indeed, of the very project of seeking to provide a theodicy – becomes sufficiently well motivated.

Sketching some of the historical milestones of antitheodicist thinking as well as the most important contemporary arguments for antitheodicism, I will suggest that antitheodicy is not only a viable option in the discourse on evil and suffering but, much more strongly, *the only decent philosophical approach to suffering* and that theodicies are, hence, incompatible with ethical seriousness to begin with. This is primarily because theodicies tend to instrumentalize innocent suffering in the service of some imagined overall good, or a metaphysical scheme failing to recognize the individual perspective of the victim of suffering. The significance of this essentially ethical argument against theodicies reaches far beyond the philosophy of religion, as the theodicy versus antitheodicy opposition can be shown to take interesting secular varieties, also having obvious political relevance in contemporary societies.

---

1 See, e.g., Rowe 2001; Meister and Moser 2017; Sterba 2017. On the complex history of the concept of evil, see, e.g., Chignell 2019a. The present book cannot engage with the question of what evil is, or how the concept ought to be defined, but we should recognize that scholars disagree on the usefulness of that notion (cf. Bernstein 2002, 2005; Card 2002; Cole 2006; and several historical analyses in Chignell 2019a). Basically, everything I have to say about antitheodicy could be said by merely speaking of suffering rather than evil, but I do believe that we need something like the concept of evil – some concept performing its role – to describe actions and events we find particularly hard to accommodate with any ordinary moral and natural understanding.

1.1. Responding to the Argument from Evil

The traditional theodicy problem is still predominantly discussed within theology and the philosophy of religion. Since antiquity, philosophers and theologians have wondered how an omnipotent, omniscient, and absolutely benevolent God (if there is such a deity) could allow the world to contain horrendous evil and suffering. Classical theodicies seek to show why God may justifiably, or at least morally excusably, create and maintain a world with such suffering. As generally recognized by philosophers writing on evil, an early articulation of the issue is the biblical *Book of Job*, whose protagonist challenges the justice of the divine world-order when faced with unmerited and purposeless suffering; it is, indeed, easy to view the *Book of Job* as an early reflection on antitheodicy (see, e.g., Dahl 2019), even though it can hardly be denied that there is significant theodicist thinking at work in the book as well (cf. Illman 2003).

The problem of evil and suffering, formulated along these primarily theological lines, is not only historically significant but continues to be actively debated within the philosophy of religion. The standard formulations of theodicies, even today, seek to respond to the atheist argument from evil challenging classical theism based on the concepts of divine omnipotence, omniscience, and absolute goodness. Because there is so much evil and suffering in the world – at least partly, or even to a significant degree, apparently entirely absurd and without purpose – there can, according to this argument, be no God that possesses those traditional attributes. If God cannot remove (unnecessary) evil, he is not omnipotent; if he is unaware of it, he is not omniscient; and if he both knows about it and could remove it (or could have created a world without that kind of evil and suffering) but does not (and did not) do so, he fails to be wholly good. While this argument from evil can be traced to antiquity, its best-known modern version was formulated in the eighteenth century by David Hume, whose criticism particularly strongly focuses on the idea that the world is "well designed," thus entangling theodicies with the traditional "design argument" seeking to demonstrate God's existence on the grounds that everything seems to function purposively in the universe.[2] Even

---

2 While something like the theodicy discussion can indeed be found in antiquity, especially Epicureanism (see, e.g., von Stosch 2013), its natural historical "home" is the early modern period. See Neiman 2002 and van der Lugt 2021 for widely appreciated historical investigations of the problem of evil and suffering in early modern philosophy, including theodicists like G.W. Leibniz and their critics like Voltaire and Hume. The arguments based on the problem of evil presented by these philosophers critical of received views on religion were revived in twentieth-century philosophy by critics of

though theodicies, as such, do not presuppose any particular "proof" of God's existence, they go naturally together with the general idea that we live in a well-ordered universe whose purposive functioning is guaranteed by a divine will. Evil and suffering are, at most, disturbances within this properly functioning world-order – and as such they need to be either explained away or put in their place as parts of God's divine scheme. As we will see later, secular theodicies[3] replace the divine will and its purposes with some non-theological proxy, such as the purposiveness of history.

Both classical and more recent as well as contemporary philosophers of religion – mostly in the monotheistic Judeo-Christian tradition[4] – have developed sophisticated analytic responses to the argument from evil. For example, medieval philosophical theologians can generally be said to have adopted either an "accidental" or an "instrumental" strategy in dealing with the problem of evil (see Posti 2019): evil is either a mere unintended consequence of good things (i.e., some evil follows from the goods that God created) or something that God may instrumentally use for good purposes (i.e., something good follows from evil). Whereas traditional theodicies attempt to provide morally acceptable reasons for God's having created a world containing evil and suffering, more moderate "mere defenses" claim to shift the burden of proof back to the atheist by suggesting that, for all we know, such reasons *might* be God's reasons (see, e.g., Plantinga 1977, 2000; van Inwagen 2006). The most widely discussed theodicy arguments (and their "mere defense" variants) include the *free will theodicy* (or defense), the *soul-making theodicy* (or defense), and the Leibnizian *"best possible world" theodicy* (or defense) – none of which will be considered in any great detail in this volume. Among such theodicies, the free will theodicy is an example of the idea that evil and suffering are unavoidable side effects of something good (i.e., free will), while soul-making theodicies emphasize the converse idea that something good

---

theism such as Mackie (1955). For a discussion of the "modernity" of theodicy in relation to the ancient versions of theodicy available in biblical literature, see Sarot 2003. For extensive scholarship on such biblical theodicies, which in many cases – e.g., in the prophets and wisdom literature – seek to legitimize the various catastrophes faced by the Israelites in terms of some kind of just divine punishment, see the essays in Laato and de Moor 2003; cf. also Newsom 2019.

3 The concept of secular theodicy has been used previously by (among others) van der Lugt (2021, 182).

4 Theodicy figures as an important theme whose relevance is not restricted to Abrahamic monotheistic religions in Max Weber's famous sociology of religion (see Weber 1956 [1922], chapter IX); Weber's work can more generally be considered an important source for sociological extensions of (secular) theodicies.

(e.g., an opportunity for spiritual growth) follows from the existence of evil and suffering.

Already Augustine suggested that God's having created human beings with free will explains why God allows evil. Later Leibniz – to whom we owe the modern idea of theodicy – maintained, in his *Théodicée* (1710), that God could not have created any better world than the one that he, as omnipotent and omnibenevolent, did create and that we therefore live in the best possible world. The world does contain some evil (perhaps even a lot), which is, however, necessary for the whole. What is common to all these lines of argument is that some X (e.g., free will, the overall goodness of creation, or the possibility of spiritual growth) is claimed to be God's actual or potential reason for creating and maintaining a world which contains apparently meaningless suffering – and that, therefore, such suffering, though real, is not entirely "meaningless," after all (viz., its meaninglessness is, indeed, merely apparent).[5]

One of the key messages of this book is that the problem of evil and suffering is not confined to theological contexts and survives the collapse of theism as a shared cultural framework.[6] At the current stage of the theodicy discussion, we must, I believe, move far beyond the traditional exclusively theological understanding of the debate by emphasizing the extremely broad relevance of the theodicy issue. By extrapolation, what we may call a "theodicist logic" is identifiable across a wide range of non-religious and non-theological contexts – in political decision-making and administration, public media and social media discussions, literature and the arts, and in principle any social practices and institutions that involve some response to suffering (as, presumably, virtually all of our social institutions in one way or another do). What is common to such patterns of thought is the explicit or implicit attempt to render other human beings' (or non-human beings') suffering

---

5 For important recent contributions (both theodicist and antitheodicist) to the theodicy debate and its assessment, critically exploring these and other theodicies and defenses, see, e.g., Bernstein 2002; Gellman et al. 2018; van Inwagen 2006; Meister and Moser 2017; Nagasawa 2024; Neiman 2002; Rowe 2001; Sterba 2017; Trakakis 2013, 2017, 2018, 2021; Wiertz 2021a, 2021b. Some of these sources will be briefly revisited in due course.
6 By this I do not exactly mean, however, what Yujin Nagasawa (2024) means when arguing that the problem of evil is a problem for atheists and naturalists at least as much (or even more) than for theists. I agree with Nagasawa that the problem is indeed everyone's problem, but I find his articulation of it dependent on the overall theodicy framework I am approaching very critically. Nagasawa brilliantly shows, however, how even the atheist holding only modestly "optimist" views on the world and the meaningfulness of existence runs into the problem of evil.

justified, excusable, or meaningful in terms of some "common good" that it serves or might serve, or in relation to which it is to be conceived of as a mere unpleasant side effect. Any overt or covert instrumentalization of suffering in the service of real or imagined overall goodness may be claimed to be quasi-theodicist, even if it has nothing to do with religious or theological attempts to explain or justify suffering.[7]

Later in the book, I will provide some obvious (and perhaps not-so-obvious) examples of secular theodicy.[8] In the interest of countering our reliance on theodicist logic in both secular and theological contexts, I will develop and defend an antitheodicist approach utilizing both *pragmatist* and *transcendental* argumentation (which I have articulated on a number of earlier occasions). What emerges, I hope, is a defense of antitheodicism as not only intellectually and ethically more plausible than theodicism but, more profoundly, as a necessary condition for the possibility of taking a seriously ethical stance to the world. I will, ultimately, claim that the theodicist is not so much wrong about how things are (e.g., about how it might or might not be possible to justify evil) but has an illusory picture of how we need to relate to how things are.

It might be asked why I have chosen to introduce antitheodicy by *defending* it, instead of aiming at a maximally neutral presentation listening equally to the different parties to the debate. My short response to this question is that the choice to employ the concept of antitheodicy in the first place is already a critical gesture. Just as one cannot really introduce ethics neutrally by describing the different ethical approaches there are as if they were products you can pick up at a supermarket if you wish, one can hardly introduce antitheodicy and antitheodicism as responses to the problem of evil and suffering in such a quasi-neutral manner, either. The very assumption of there being a neutral perspective available for such an introduction is something that can (and, I think, should) be criticized by invoking the concept of antitheodicy. The *seriousness* of the matter under discussion cannot be communicated

---

7 The need to consider the relations between religious/theological and secular approaches to the problem of evil has of course been recognized previously (for some discussion, see Pihlström 2019). However, in such discussions it is typically assumed that theodicies only operate within the religious/theological discourse, and one aim of this book is to argue that this assumption must be abandoned. Indirectly, taking secular theodicies and their criticism seriously, we may also respond to those who believe the entire vocabulary of "evil" to be dated (e.g., Cole 2006; Chignell 2019a). Continuing to speak of evil and to explore the problems of theodicist thinking is, in my view, a way of taking our moral predicament seriously.

8 As an illustrative case study, I will, among other things, explore the ways in which both the just war theory and pacifism seem to operate in terms of a theodicist logic (see Chapter 5).

by pretending to be able to avoid taking a stand to the different views debating against one another. I will, however, investigate the meta-level problem of how exactly it is possible to argue for antitheodicism (and what it means to do so) in Chapters 5 and 6.

What I am hoping to introduce in this book, then, is an inherently *critical* endeavor. However, this also entails *self-critical* vigilance: we should never simply rest satisfied with the concept of antitheodicy we have chosen to employ but ought to examine its potential problems and incoherences as meticulously as possible. Accordingly, one of the questions that will come up in Chapter 5 is whether we can avoid the "return" of theodicy. An introduction to antitheodicy is, then, inevitably also an attempt to develop a sufficiently rich and morally sensitive philosophical language for speaking of the darkest moments of human life and our shared history, that is, for acknowledging the reality of suffering. Such an introduction cannot be a neutral (supermarket-like) comparison of different views as if they were all on par but must be a committed attempt to navigate the thicket of those views by developing such an ethically responsible language that is as adequate for this task as possible. Here it is easy to follow Mara van der Lugt's (2021, 405) advise: "It *matters* how we speak of suffering, because speaking *of* suffering is always speaking *to* suffering as well." I will argue that the theodicist logic is an ethically problematic way of speaking of, as well as to, suffering – and that there is a sense in which it is, therefore, not genuinely "available" to us (not to be "picked up" at a value-neutral supermarket, to continue the analogy) within any serious ethical framework.

1.2. The Plan of the Book

This book will provide not as much an overview of the problem of evil and suffering, or of standard theodicist ways of approaching that problem, as an introduction to the ethical significance of the antitheodicist alternative to that mainstream discussion.[9] My task is to try to explain why a substantial examination of antitheodicy is needed and what the main contribution of antitheodicism to the relevant research field(s) is. While I will not aim at a neutral exposition of different ways of thinking but at an argument defending antitheodicism, the book also gives a fair hearing to forms of theodicism. I will introduce antitheodicy by critically engaging with historical and contemporary

---

9 As noted, for discussions of traditional and contemporary theodicies (or "defenses"), the reader may consult various introductions and companions to the philosophy of religion, for instance, or specifically to the problem of evil.

philosophical literature on the problem of evil and suffering, but I try to do this without presupposing detailed knowledge of the topic.

After this introduction, Chapter 2 provides some important conceptual background for the subsequent chapters, distinguishing (in some more detail than this introductory chapter) between theodicy and antitheodicy, theodicism and antitheodicism, as well as religious/theological and secular approaches to the topic. Importantly, the debate between theodicism and antitheodicism must be carefully distinguished from the one between theism and atheism; typically, an atheist is a "theodicist" in the sense of presupposing the *normative* requirement that theism ought to deliver a theodicy. Antitheodicism (in my sense) rejects not only specific theodicies but this requirement itself, that is, the very project of trying to provide a theodicy. Its relations to other disputes in the philosophy of religion – especially those between realism and antirealism, on the one hand, and evidentialism and fideism, on the other – will also be briefly spelled out. Furthermore, the basic idea of "secular theodicy" will be critically introduced in this context, and the wide significance of antitheodicism – extending, as suggested, far beyond the philosophy of religion – will thereby be emphasized. Moreover, the theodicism versus antitheodicism debate will be compared to the better-known opposition between optimism and pessimism (given the obvious association of theodicies and optimism), but the latter will be rearticulated to include the critical middle-ground option provided by "meliorism."

Chapter 3 offers a brief historical sketch of the development of antitheodicist thought. While the term "antitheodicy" was at least in its current meaning explicitly introduced rather late – as has often been noted, by Zachary Braiterman in 1998[10] – the ethical critique of theodicies is as old as the *Book of Job*. Drawing from relevant scholarship on the history of early modern philosophy, in particular (by Susan Neiman and Mara van der Lugt, among others),[11] the chapter shows how antitheodicies emerge from critiques of Enlightenment optimism, culminating in Immanuel Kant's 1791 Theodicy Essay (especially its remarkable reading of the *Book of Job*) and Arthur Schopenhauer's famous pessimism. No extensive historical interpretations of these or other classical thinkers can be provided in a brief treatment of the matter, but the historical layers of the (anti)theodicy

---

10 In fact, the term "antitheodicy" occurs earlier, at least in Berckman's (1976) analysis of Bertolt Brecht's struggles with the Christian tradition (though perhaps not exactly in the same meaning as in Braiterman's and his followers' work).

11 See Neiman 2002 and van der Lugt 2021 – the two most important historical investigations of early modern developments in the theodicy versus antitheodicy controversies (cf. also Neiman 2019).

discussion need to be recognized in order to get an adequate picture of the topic. The chapter rather quickly turns to more recent history, however, exploring antitheodicist ideas in twentieth-century philosophy and emphasizing the antitheodicist aspects of three apparently quite different orientations in ethics and the philosophy of religion: pragmatism (especially William James), Wittgensteinian moral philosophy (e.g., D.Z. Phillips), and Levinasian ethics of otherness. It will be argued that these antitheodicist approaches are equally relevant in religious/theological and secular contexts (thus re-emphasizing the importance of secular theodicies and their ethical critique) and that pragmatist antitheodicism, in particular, offers an original articulation of meliorism as an alternative to both optimism and pessimism. Pragmatism can thus, in a way, be used as a meta-theory coordinating the "use" of other antitheodicies, such as Wittgenstein- or Levinas-inspired ones – that is, putting them into relevant uses in different contexts.

It needs to be examined, however, whether a stable meliorist antitheodicism is possible: insofar as the pessimist critique of theodicist optimism is taken seriously (even when developing meliorism), can pessimism in the end be avoided without succumbing to the "temptations of theodicy" (borrowing a term from Levinas, emphasized by, e.g., Richard Bernstein's reading of his antitheodicism)? Does antitheodicism even entail the darkest kind of pessimism defended by "antinatalists" who maintain that the world is so full of suffering that it would be better for sentient beings not to exist at all – and if so, is this a *reductio ad absurdum* of antitheodicism? Can the antitheodicist find any meaning in historical events or in life in general? Questions such as these lead us to the treatment of contemporary varieties of antitheodicism in Chapter 4, which also contains an extensive discussion of the ethics of war and peace from the perspective of the theodicy versus antitheodicy issue. Grounded in the overview provided in Chapter 3, the articulation of contemporary secular antitheodicism in Chapter 4 will primarily utilize a pragmatist methodology of evaluating the potential practical significance of philosophical positions in our individual and social lives.

Chapter 5 takes a step onto the meta-level by arguing that antitheodicism is constitutive of what we may call ethical seriousness – and thus, in the end, of the very possibility of occupying an ethical stance at all. It will be suggested that our ethical critique of theodicies remains naïve if construed merely as a "moralizing" critique according to which theodicies are simply morally wrong. (Examples of such views will be provided.) A philosophically more profound version of ethical antitheodicism thus takes a Kant-inspired transcendental shape: antitheodicism ought to be understood as a *necessary condition for the possibility of ethics*, or as *constitutive of the meaning of the ethical* for us in this world of suffering.¹² This idea, captured in the phrase "transcendental antitheodicism," will be developed in the chapter by borrowing an important concept from Raimond Gaita (2004 [1991]): "the unthinkable." It will be proposed that theodicies should be regarded as "unthinkable" in the sense that they cannot even be (seriously) ethically considered as responses to suffering, that is, as responses that could possibly be ethically acceptable.¹³ On the contrary, they lead us beyond ethics, even if they are ethically well-intended.¹⁴ However (and this, I suppose, is one of the novelties of the argument of this book in comparison to the results achieved in my earlier research on these topics), even this line of thought must be problematized. We may ask whether antitheodicism is itself a necessary (or, in Kantian terms, transcendental) condition for the possibility of the kind of ethical seriousness that needs to be already in place for us to be so much as able to distinguish between the ethically "unthinkable" and the (thinkable but) "merely wrong." If this were the case, then we would hardly be able to claim theodicies to be unthinkable, after all; the latter concept, with the moral seriousness it incorporates, would be available to us only insofar as we had *already* rejected theodicism. The chapter tentatively proposes that antitheodicism and the ethical seriousness manifested by our distinguishing between what is merely wrong (though thinkable) and what is unthinkable (viz., what cannot even be decently considered) are "reciprocally contained" in each other, presupposing one another and thus functioning as elements of a holistic understanding of the meaning of "the ethical" in our lives. Chapter 5 also contains some further case studies on secular theodicism and antitheodicism, particularly regarding historical meaning(fulness),¹⁵ hopefully further indicating the extremely broad relevance of our topic.

---

12 I will not claim that this would have been Kant's own view, though. My antitheodicism is "Kantian" only in a broad sense of taking its inspiration, and transcendental (albeit also pragmatic) methodology, from Kant.

13 I discuss and further develop Gaita's concept of the unthinkable from a variety of perspectives in Pihlström 2025.

14 That they might be, and often are, must not be overlooked. In short, we should, even at our most critical, never simply condemn theodicies. We should value their background motivation of understanding evil and suffering – often in a theistic context, as manifested in biblical theodicies (see Laato and de Moor 2003) – while firmly rejecting what emerges from that motivation. Moreover, it must be kept in mind that atheist criticism of theodicies (which is not antitheodicist in my sense because it does not reject the theodicist logic itself) is often also deeply morally serious (see, e.g., Shook 2016).

15 In this regard, the book also connects with recent debates within the philosophy of history and historiography or of the humanities generally (cf. Pihlström 2022).

The concluding Chapter 6 pulls the threads together and briefly explains why the results achieved, especially those of Chapter 5, are widely relevant to our lives in contemporary societies. I will also re-emphasize, by way of conclusion, what is really at stake in this entire discussion – namely, the very meaning of "the ethical."

Chapter 2
CONCEPTUAL AND METHODOLOGICAL PRELIMINARIES

Introducing antitheodicy and antitheodicism obviously requires understanding what "theodicy" is. The purpose of this chapter is to provide necessary conceptual preliminaries, especially regarding the distinctions between theodicy and antitheodicy, theodicism and antitheodicism, religious/theological and secular approaches, as well as optimism, pessimism, and meliorism. An overview of these ideas is needed for the purposes of the subsequent chapters, which will offer historical interpretations of key forms of antitheodicy and reflections on the contemporary relevance of antitheodicist thinking. In order to specify the relevant conceptual distinctions, I will, however, begin with some examples that also motivate methodological reflection.

2.1. Justifying Suffering

The justification or legitimation of others' suffering need not be – and often isn't – religious at all, even though classical theodicies are attempts to defend theism in a world of evil and suffering. Real-life cases of *secular theodicies* at work are not difficult to find. For example, when debating (as we all did in 2020–22) along largely utilitarian lines whether societies ought to introduce heavy restrictions in order to prevent the uncontrolled spread of Covid-19 infections, it might be argued (and *was* widely argued during the pandemic) that because the virus is in most cases fatal only to the elderly and other medical risk groups, the "common good" requires that the restrictions are not too demanding. According to such arguments, sacrificing the smooth functioning of the economy by preventing as many deaths as possible would be worse, all things considered, than letting some potential victims (especially the elderly and individuals belonging to the medical risk groups) die, as "they would die anyway." This crudely utilitarian line of thought instrumentalizes Covid-19 victims' hardships to overall benefits at the societal level, thus arguably employing a broadly "theodicist" logic in excusing their suffering. The welfare of all (or, at least, of many) is thus considered an allegedly morally acceptable reason for allowing the sufferings and even deaths of some. The logic is strikingly analogous to, say, that of the religious free will theodicist who claims that the reason why God may allow even horrible suffering such as the Holocaust is (for example) the fact that a world inhabited by human beings with free will is, despite the Holocaust horrors, far better, all things considered, than a world without freedom and responsibility would be.[1]

Conversely, however, a theodicist logic may also be claimed to have been at work in the context of the Covid-19 pandemic when restaurants and other services were closed, and thousands of people lost their jobs due to the restrictions: those people were also instrumentalized in the service of what was taken to be the common good. Their losses enabled saving lives. Examples like this show how justifying others' suffering is at the heart of various social institutions and practices. Almost anything we do when instituting and maintaining any social norms and practices requires some balancing of "costs" and "benefits," and often these become concretely manifested in terms of some (implicit, if not explicit) "price" that we are prepared (and may argue that everyone ought to be prepared) to "pay" in the form of various sufferings, including lost lives, or as some accidental and unintended (even if anticipated) "by-product" that we are willing to accept (or consider, albeit unwillingly, necessary to accept).[2] Our relations to other human beings in general thus largely seem to operate in terms of implicit secular theodicies. In most cases, these patterns of thought are, indeed, secular, as neither religious beliefs nor any theological theorizations need to be involved. It is almost unavoidable for us to (to a degree) "justify" others' suffering whenever discussing, for example, which political decisions might be the most beneficial or the least harmful for most of us. Such discussion almost inevitably utilizes some form of utilitarian logic, maximizing benefits and minimizing costs (viz., suffering). While utilitarianism may not directly entail theodicy, and theodicist logic need not be utilitarian, a perfect example of theodicist thinking at work is the – often politically inescapable – utilitarian excusing of suffering with reference to overall goods and benefits. For example, public social and health-care services may have to be cut down in an economically challenging situation, and this will cause suffering to many, especially the poor and the sick, but the "overall benefit" of maintaining a welfare society even in the future by secur-

---

1 For an exploration of Covid-19 and theodicy, see Pihlström and Kivistö 2023, Chapter 3.
2 See, e.g., Scarry 1987 for a critical analysis of the notion of suffering as a "by-product" (e.g., in the context of war).

ing its financial basis will ultimately justify even severe austerity measures – or so a politician may argue. Given the practical necessity of operating along such quasi-theodicist lines in political decision-making by seeking maximal benefit and minimal costs, it is essential to uncover the structures of theodicist thinking also in secular contexts, even if we can never fully liberate ourselves from them.[3]

The metaphor of "price" suggests a quasi-objective scale on which we can "measure" different sufferings as well as the possible benefits they might be taken to be prices for. Accordingly, the theodicist logic in its various guises can be claimed to assume that sufferings are in principle not only measurable but also commensurate, meaningfully comparable to one another. It seems that presupposing such measurability (and commensurability) is necessary for the idea of justifying or excusing the reality of suffering, because the very project of justification must operate in terms of some in principle comparable goods or benefits that can be contrasted with harms and losses. The critic of theodicism thus suggests that the idea of such measurement – and the idea of comparing the "results" of different measurements, like different prices for some relevantly similar products – is ethically reprehensible or possibly even unthinkable given the sense of "immeasurability" that we (may or perhaps ought to) attach to experiences of suffering. To treat a person's sincere suffering experience as incommensurable with other such experiences is to treat that person as an individual deserving unconditional respect and recognition, even if we in the end disagree with them regarding, say, the causes and nature of their suffering.[4]

Even when not religious, the alleged justification (utilitarian or not) of others' pain often takes place from a totalizing "God's-Eye View" – an overarching absolute perspective attributing some meaning or purpose to the suffering – that remains unavailable to the victim of suffering themselves occupying an individual limited perspective. Hence, the key assumption of theodicy is not simply trivially reducible to the obvious fact that all our practices have unintended side effects ("double effects," "by-products"). It is, rather, constituted by the idea that there is, albeit possibly hidden from us or from any particular individual, an absolute point of view on how things are and how they ought to be (at some kind of fundamental metaphysical, even if not necessarily

---

3 Therefore, it is good to keep in mind throughout this discussion – though this will become explicit only in the concluding Chapter 6 – that the fundamental issue regarding antitheodicy is the nature of the ethical. We are primarily engaging in ethical – not political, not theological, not religious – argumentation in this book.

4 For an insightful articulation of antitheodicism in terms of the conceptual machinery of gifts and burdens, highlighting the immeasurability of suffering, see Saarinen 2019.

theological, level) and that this absolute standpoint also places individual experiences of apparently meaningless suffering into their proper perspective, possibly even yielding "measures" for comparing and "pricing" them. What is essential to theodicies is precisely this explicit or implicit postulation of an overarching justificatory perspective, rather than theistic metaphysics as such.

In our current global circumstances of war and conflict, a worsening climate crisis, geopolitical and economic tensions, and increasing insecurity about the future of liberal democracies, secular extrapolations of theodicies become even more urgent. Writing in the aftermath of the catastrophic sufferings of the twentieth century, Emmanuel Levinas (2006 [1982]), one of the leading ethical thinkers of the past century, famously noted that theodicy – the justification of another human being's suffering – is "the source of all immorality."[5] Similarly, Richard Bernstein (2002) repeatedly referred to the "obscenity" of theodicy in his writings on evil.[6] It is easy to join these and other ethical critics of theodicy when reading, for example, the kind of justifications of suffering we find in Richard Swinburne's work, such as his suggestion that by allowing slavery to occur, God provided both slaves and slave owners with situations for moral growth, including opportunities to enable others' growth (see Swinburne 1998, 245).[7]

Taking critical comments by thinkers like Levinas and Bernstein seriously, it must be asked whether our relations to other human beings are *inevitably* based on ethically problematic theodicist assumptions. The examples raised above demonstrate that theodicies have – borrowing a simile from Hannah Arendt's (1994 [1963]) famous conceptualization of the "banality of evil" – a tendency of spreading like a "fungus" with no center: theodicies need no metaphysical, theological, or religious core, and they can occupy virtually any area of (also fully secular) thought and action. Obvious examples of secular theodicies include Hegelian and Marxist views on historical teleology; indeed, many leading twentieth-century intellectuals' morally catastrophic communist odysseys were grounded in the illusion that historical events must have a deeper "meaning" (see Judt 1992; this example will be briefly discussed in Chapter 5). However, there are many other kinds of secular theodicy around, including the politically very different claim that what justifies

---

5 While this book is not a close study of Levinas, we will return to this remark in Chapters 3 and 5.
6 See Bernstein 2002, especially the chapter on Levinas.
7 This example is discussed in Echazú's (2024b) analysis of the problematic way in which Swinburne employs "ideal" theorizing in his theodicy-construction. Swinburne (1998) combines different theodicies in his overall account, whereas Hick (2010 [1966]) is the most famous proponent (in modern philosophy of religion) of the "soul-making theodicy" justifying suffering in terms of moral or spiritual growth.

historical suffering is not the unfolding of some quasi-Hegelian historical *telos* but the goods delivered to all (or, at least, to most) by the maximally unrestricted functioning of free markets, even if some (or many) of us will have no proper share of those goods. The temptation of secular theodicy can, thus, take diverging political shapes.

There is a lot of work that should be done on theodicies in general and secular theodicies in particular in order to analyze these conceptual assumptions and to subject them to ethical critique. Such discussions may build upon the analytic work going on in the philosophy of religion but need not continue to debate on the credentials of theism and atheism, and thus need not directly contribute to the traditional theological theodicy debate at all. There is little to be achieved in that area, I believe, as the basic positions and argument strategies have been firmly established, and there seems to be no shared view on what would even constitute progress in the argumentation for and against theodicies (or for and against theism in relation to theodicy). Instead, more general ethical examination of theodicies is, essentially, an engagement in secular critical philosophy (including the philosophy of religion, conceived of as a secular enterprise) by identifying a previously unrecognized theodicist pattern in a number of contexts that have fundamental ethical and political relevance to our contemporary world. This theodicist logic needs to be revealed and subjected to thoroughgoing critical assessment. For this purpose, it is important to develop an antitheodicist approach, partly based on the insights of leading critics of theodicy (see Chapter 3) representing a variety of original philosophical outlooks. It is my main task in this volume to outline such an approach and to provide arguments for finding it superior to the theodicist one. More concrete "applied" work tackling issues of contemporary societies in more detail along antitheodicist lines must be left to others.

2.2. Challenging the Justificatory Project: Methodological Remarks

Antitheodicism, in the sense in which I will develop it here, rejects not merely particular theodicy arguments but the theodicist *presuppositions* of the debate on the problem of evil and suffering. I am thus in basic agreement with Nick Trakakis (2013), who characterizes antitheodicy as the outright rejection – on moral or some other philosophical grounds – of all theodicist attempts to discern God's reasons for permitting evil. The antitheodicist approach seems to be receiving increased attention today,[8] and the ethical criticism of theodicy

---

[8] See, e.g., Gleeson 2012; Betenson 2016; Trakakis 2013, 2017, 2018, 2021; Schönbaumsfeld 2021; Snellman 2023; Echazú 2024a.

can be argued to be something that should be taken seriously also by scholars subscribing to, or at least continuing to discuss, (relatively) traditional forms of theism, finding antitheodicy arguments relevant to the assessment of the theism versus atheism debate.[9]

The relations between ethical antitheodicy finding theodicies morally problematic and an allegedly more basic "conceptual" antitheodicy based on a critique of the (meta)metaphysical background assumptions of theodicism also need to be further investigated. While I cannot in this book respond in any detail to Lauri Snellman's (2023) brilliant articulation of what he labels conceptual antitheodicy[10] – something that he takes to be primary to any "merely" moral antitheodicy – I will examine in Chapter 5 the *ethical seriousness* of antitheodicism by suggesting that the conceptual and the ethical are deeply entangled. One of my aims is to argue that antitheodicism, even when primarily ethically oriented, should not be simply moral (let alone moralizing or moralistic) but should recognize the dependence of our practices of ethical engagement and discussion on the acknowledgment of the unacceptability, or even "unthinkability," of theodicist excuses for evil and suffering as allegedly something that exists (according to an overarching divine scheme) because of some "greater good." This dependence is itself ethical but also "conceptual."

On the other hand, it is worth emphasizing already at this early stage of our discussion that maintaining a critical distance from straightforwardly "moralizing" antitheodicies is not to move beyond the moral sphere. This observation is of utmost methodological importance for our inquiry. Our need to think carefully about the meaning of the ethical in our lives – which, I will argue, entails understanding antitheodicism as a constitutive condition of moral seriousness – is itself an ethical project that can, or perhaps should, encompass our entire lives. Antitheodicism, as a challenge to the entire justificatory project of theodicies, will thus inevitably be a form of moral critique even when it avoids making direct moral judgments. Moreover, it would be hard to completely avoid such judgments, or even downright moral horror, when faced by some of the most straightforward pronouncements by theodicists who speculate about, for example, the possibility that God may have acted justifiably in providing opportunities for moral and spiritual growth for slaves and slave owners (or Jews and Nazis) by allowing slavery and the

---

9 Cf. Simpson 2009; Shearn 2013; Franklin 2020.
10 I am also indebted to some of Snellman's unpublished article manuscripts on antitheodicy. Note that those who emphasize the predominantly moral aspects of antitheodicist critiques of theodicy may admit that one can also have good metaphysical reasons for rejecting theodicies (see Trakakis 2017).

Holocaust to happen, because the existence of such opportunities for us to employ our freedom is such a good thing that we just have to accept even horrible sufferings in return.[11] Methodologically, the crucial point here is that a conceptual critique focusing on the conditions of morality may *eo ipso* amount to ethical critique.

In general, antitheodicy remains (even after this book) to be much more systematically articulated and applied to debates on what it means to respond ethically and politically to suffering beyond theological contexts. While "secular theodicy" may still sound like an oxymoron, the above-described striking analogies between the classical theodicy issue and the non-theological manifestations of justifying or excusing others' suffering deserve detailed philosophical attention. Investigating these issues may serve both theoretical and practical goals: nothing less than the foundations of justice in contemporary societies are at stake in antitheodicist critique, just as the justice of the divine creation is questioned by Job.

While many scholars have loosely referred to secular analogies of theodicies, no general systematic treatment of theodicism as a general position reaching beyond the philosophy of religion exists. Accordingly, no systematic philosophical articulation or defense of what I am calling antiheodicism exists, either – prior to this introduction. One conceptual novelty to be proposed in these discussions is that the distinction between theodicism and antitheodicism is *normative* both are taken to govern the ways in which the problem of evil and suffering ought to be discussed and inquired into. Thus, an atheist can be, and usually is, a theodicist in the sense of expecting the theist to deliver a theodicy, albeit failing (and similarly, *mutatis mutandis*, for secular theodicies). Antitheodicism thus needs to be constructed as an irreducibly normative stance constraining our responses to suffering. This requires a critical analysis of the ethical presuppositions and implications of both theodicism and antitheodicism.

Furthermore, what is needed in an inquiry like this is a solid philosophical methodology for developing the relevant arguments challenging the justificatory aims of theodicies. I have previously argued for *transcendental antitheodicism* as a novel approach to the problem of evil and suffering (see, e.g., Pihlström 2020a, 2023, 2025, as well as Chapter 5). "Transcendental" must here be understood in its Kantian sense, referring to an investigation of the necessary

---

11 This is only a very simplified version of the so-called soul-making theodicy (cf. Hick 2010 [1966]; Swinburne 1998), and I am not pretending to do justice to any of its specific versions. It is only the general idea whose moral status may and should be questioned.

conditions for the possibility of something that is regarded as an actual element of our practices (e.g., cognition, meaning, or – in this case – an ethical stance to others or what was above described as ethical seriousness). The transcendental antitheodicist maintains that antitheodicism is necessary for the possibility of adequately ethically recognizing the perspective(s) of the victim(s) of suffering and their understanding of the meaninglessness of their suffering. Such recognition is, arguably, necessary for the possibility of ethical sincerity or even for finding something a matter of serious moral concern. While this line of thought – to be more carefully discussed in Chapter 5 – falls in the general category of ethical antitheodicism, it operates at a transcendental level because it does not simply defend antitheodicism as the morally correct view (or charge theodicies of a "first-order" moral failure) but as a constitutive condition of our practices of ethical argumentation and deliberation.[12] As the focus is on the conditions of human practices, this transcendental argumentation is *ipso facto* pragmatic. This general pragmatist-cum-transcendental argument must, however, be critically evaluated, specified, and further developed in the discussions concerning secular theodicies and their critique in different contexts.

Developing such a critical approach to theodicism implicit in our practices (including secular practices) can thus be seen as not only a Kant-inspired transcendental proposal but also a *pragmatist* move, given that pragmatism – the philosophical orientation initiated by Charles S. Peirce, William James, and John Dewey in the United States in the late nineteenth century – urges us to examine the meanings of our concepts and theories in terms of the conceivable practical effects of their objects.[13] The kind of critical (transcendental) inquiry into the practice-laden, irreducibly ethical meaning of (anti)theodicism that I am claiming we need is thus ultimately grounded in pragmatism. For this reason, pragmatism will function as a kind of meta-theory for my articulation of transcendental antitheodicism in the next chapters (especially

---

12 We should read the above-cited Levinasian phrase about theodicies being the source of all immorality as not claiming that theodicies *per se* are immoral (i.e., not as a moralizing statement at all) but as, indeed, claiming that various immoralities have their underlying sources, or roots, in theodicism. (In Kantian terms, theodicies could thus be taken to be "radically evil," understanding the word "radical" in its etymological sense referring to "root," Lat. *radix*.) See Pöykkö 2023 for a recent reading of Levinas as a transcendental ethical thinker.

13 On pragmatism in the philosophy of religion, see, e.g., Pihlström 2013; cf. Pihlström 2024. Among classical pragmatists, James's commitment to antitheodicism – without using this term – is particularly clear: see James 1975 [1907], Lectures I and VIII, as well as Chapter 3.

Chapters 4 and 5). Pragmatism also enables us to maintain a meliorist view in contrast to both optimism and pessimism. While optimism is the typical background idea of theodicies and theodicism, uncritically suggesting that the world is "good" in some overall sense, the antitheodicist need not settle for the pessimist extreme, either, but can subscribe to, and argue for, the critical middle-ground option known as meliorism.

The articulation and defense of antitheodicism in this study will, thus, employ a combination of pragmatist and transcendental methodologies serving both ethical and conceptual critique. My actual use of these methods will, however, only emerge in the subsequent chapters as we will deal with the substantial questions of our inquiry.

2.3. The Basic Concepts

Having tentatively introduced the most important concepts and methods that need to be at our disposal in the discussion that follows, let me simply list the key concepts to be employed. Note that the following are not universally accepted definitions but inevitably somewhat loose characterizations of how I have chosen to use those concepts in this book (and in my earlier work). In particular, the word "theodicy" itself has received different meanings during its history (see Sarot 2003),[14] and a short introduction like this cannot possibly cover the variety of uses of even its central concepts.

Theodicies are arguments or argumentatively grounded theories claiming to reconcile the undeniable empirical fact of apparently meaningless suffering with a broader scheme of meaningfulness or with a life within which "meaning-making" remains possible despite horrible suffering. The scheme postulated may be, and often is, theistic, but this is not necessarily the case, because there are, as we have seen, secular theodicies in which some secular (e.g., historical-teleological or political) proxy plays the role of divine justice. Theodicies essentially *justify* or *excuse* the fact that there is suffering by appealing to either God's purposes or some kind of historical (including, e.g., economic or political) meaningfulness. They thus claim that, far from being simply meaningless, even the most horrendous suffering is useful or potentially meaningful in some way, even if it can never be recognized as such by

---

14 Some maintain that it is anachronistic to refer by "theodicy" to any discussions of evil and suffering before Leibniz (who coined the term), while others (including the contributors to Laato and de Moor 2003) believe that it makes sense to extend the historical usage of the term to cover even the ancient and biblical world. In any case, we must be aware of the historical layers of this concept – like any other heavily loaded philosophical and/or theological concept.

the victim, or at least that in the overall scheme of things we can reconcile ourselves with the reality of that suffering. Thus, in their theistic or specifically Christian employment, theodicies are typically (though not necessarily) apologetic: they seek to convince the non-believer that it is not irrational to believe in God's existence despite the horrors of the created world.

More specifically, in their core theological context, theodicies are attempts to respond to the argument from evil, which (as we saw in Chapter 1) in its traditional form proceeds from the empirical premise that there is apparently meaningless suffering and from the definition of God as omnipotent, omniscient, and omnibenevolent to the conclusion that such God cannot exist, given suffering. In this book, I am not making any heavy use of the distinction between "theodicies proper" and *mere defenses*, although the latter are more modest than the former, only suggesting some particular account of the justification or potential meaningfulness of suffering as God's (or, in principle, a secular proxy's) *possible* reason for allowing that suffering to exist. Thus, while theodicies claim that some X is, or can plausibly be regarded as, God's moral reason for allowing apparently gratuitous suffering, mere defenses only suggest that X *might*, for all we know, be such a reason (see, e.g., van Inwagen 2006).[15] Mere defenses contribute to the project of theodicy, only proposing a possible rather than actual theodicy. Yet, both are committed to seeking a theodicist justification of suffering, either actual or potential, and therefore both, when employed within an overall defense of Christian theism, for instance, are equally apologetic. For my purposes in this discussion, this distinction is not as central as it seems to be in most of the mainstream theorizations of the problem of evil in contemporary analytic philosophy of religion, in particular.

Another distinction that needs to be recognized even though it will not play any crucial role in my explorations is the one between the *logical* and the *evidential* versions of the problem of evil and suffering (see, e.g., Rowe 2001). While the former concludes that atheism logically follows from the argument from evil, the latter merely maintains that that argument presents an epistemological challenge to the theist, inviting the theist to provide counterarguments and counterevidence in response to the claim that probably there is no God, given evil and suffering.[16] In the latter formulation, the reality of

---

15 More technically, a "defense" could claim that some reason X is God's reason for permitting suffering in a possible world W and that we cannot know that our actual world is not W. Defenses are thus often connected with *skeptical theism*, according to which we should remain skeptical about God's actual reasons while endorsing theism.

16 It is, typically, in response to the evidential problem of evil that "mere defenses" are put forward; accordingly, van Inwagen (2006), among others, characterizes the

suffering is, in brief, a piece of evidence against theism. The prevalence of this discourse in the contemporary debates on evil and suffering suggests that the problem is often viewed from a broadly evidentialist standpoint, characteristic of contemporary philosophy of religion generally. Suffering is treated as an empirical premise providing a potential "defeater" to theism, and thus it plays a role in an argumentative exchange searching for evidence either in support of or against the theistic claim. I am not claiming that theodicies necessarily entail evidentialism, as there are major philosophers of religion who reject evidentialism (strictly speaking) while developing theodicies or "defenses" within, say, reformed epistemology (cf. again Plantinga 2000; van Inwagen 2006), but clearly there is an affinity between these overall views.

Antitheodicies are arguments challenging or criticizing theodicies (and, by extension, mere defenses), no matter whether they are put forward as responses to the logical or the evidential form of the argument from evil, either focusing on a particular theodicy and claiming that it does not do its job of reconciling us with suffering or arguing against theodicies in general. The task of an antitheodicy is thus essentially critical and negative. It is intended as a refutation of a theodicy or a group of theodicies (or, by extension, defenses). However, antitheodicies in this sense must be carefully distinguished from the criticism of theodicies we find in atheist arguments based on the problem of evil and suffering (arguments "from evil"), according to which it is rational to embrace atheism precisely for the reason that it would be either logically contradictory or epistemologically unjustified to maintain that an omnipotent, omniscient, and absolutely good deity would allow the suffering there undeniably is in the world. Unlike the critiques of theodicies presented by thinkers from David Hume to J.L. Mackie and beyond, antitheodicies in my sense do *not* draw this atheist conclusion, because they are not intended to participate in the argumentative game between theism and atheism in the first place.[17] They do not play the "game" of the argument from evil and the responses to it that theodicies present. On the contrary, they remind us that those who do draw the atheist conclusion from the argument from evil are themselves in the

---

debate in terms of an analogy to a courtroom case where the theist, by offering a "defense" (e.g., the "free will defense"), seeks to shift the burden of proof to the atheist who claims to challenge theism by appealing to the reality of evil and suffering.

17 Therefore, I find it misleading to discuss Hume's (1990 [1779], chapter X) or, in more recent philosophy of religion, a view like Mackie's (1955) – which is a modern classic in atheist challenges to theistic theodicies – in the context of antitheodicy, as Scott (2015, Chapter 7) does (citing Mackie), though Scott's book is important because it takes antitheodicy seriously as a distinctive response to the problem of evil along with theodicies.

grip of a theodicist logic. Accordingly, it is clearly possible to defend antitheodicies while remaining committed to, say, Jewish or Christian theism (see, e.g., Surin 1986; Roth 2004). Antitheodicies, in short, are attempts to refute what theodicies are in the business of doing, not merely their conclusions.

This brings me to the distinction between theodicism and antitheodicism, which, I am suggesting, is ethically more important than the one between theism and atheism and operates at a meta-level in comparison to the more straightforward distinction between theodicies and antitheodicies (conceived of as particular arguments or theories). *Theodicism* can be characterized as the *normative* view that the problem of evil and suffering ought to be approached with the interest of delivering a theodicy (or, more modestly, a mere defense).[18] Theodicism, then, is not necessarily committed to any particular theodicy but may utilize any of them (again, either in their classical theological or extended secular forms). However, importantly, theodicism may also lead one to conclude, negatively, that no theodicy – at least none among those presented up to now – functions or does its job. Therefore, the atheist criticizing theism on the basis of the problem of evil and suffering may be, and usually is, a theodicist in this normative sense, only arguing that the theodicist expectation (shared by the theist and the atheist) is not fulfilled and that therefore we should conclude that there is no God or that it is irrational to believe in God. (Again, this can also be formulated in terms of a secular proxy, such as our faith in the purposive meaningfulness of history.) Even more strongly, it may be suggested that atheism based on the argument from evil necessarily operates within a theodicist framework, employing the empirical premise that there is evil and suffering in an evidential role in arguing against theism.

In this broad sense, the theist putting forward some particular theodicy, or a mixture of them (e.g., free will theodicy, soul-making theodicy, or something similar), the atheist criticizing those theodicies because they fail to deliver what they promise, as well as the more modest theist only suggesting a "mere defense" in the interest of shifting the burden of proof back to the atheist, are all "theodicists." They share the normative assumption that a theodicy ought to be delivered, and they continue to debate on theism versus atheism by investigating whether or not it is or can be delivered. Accordingly, the theodicist project in contemporary philosophy of religion, and more broadly, is

---

18 Analogously, evidentialism is the normative epistemological view (in the philosophy of religion) that religious beliefs ought to be backed up by evidence, or rational considerations generally, and that the rational acceptability of religious beliefs depends on their enjoying such evidential support. For pragmatist philosophy of religion as an attempt to steer a middle course between evidentialism and its traditional opposite, fideism, see Pihlström 2013.

not restricted to those who offer us explicit theodicies (e.g., Swinburne 1998; Hick 2010 [1966]) – arguments whose history can be traced back to classical figures such as Augustine and Irenaeus (respectively) – nor to those providing mere defenses (e.g., again, Plantinga and van Inwagen), but also includes those, such as Marilyn McCord Adams (1999), who reject all standard theodicies as morally unacceptable instrumentalizing justifications of evil while continuing to appeal to a postmortem "beatific" metaphysical divine compensation for the injustices and sufferings of the empirical world, and even those atheists (e.g., Mackie 1955; Martin 1990) who seek to refute any such theodicies, concluding (within the theodic*ist* framework, as it were) that God does not exist. Moreover, importantly for the purposes of this book, the theodicist project includes all those secular thinkers who may find this entire discourse on the traditional problem of evil thoroughly outdated but continue to reflect on historical or political excuses for suffering.

Antitheodicism also operates at a normative meta-level, rejecting theodicism as a general approach to the problem of evil and suffering, arguing that we ought not to operate in terms of such an approach. Antitheodicism usually provides ethical reasons for this view, claiming that there is something ethically dubious not only in particular theodicies (or atheist arguments finding theodicies unsuccessful) but in the theodicist project itself, that is, in the normative expectation that a theodicy ought to be delivered as a response to the suffering we find around us. Thus, antitheodicism is a meta-level view in relation to specific antitheodicy arguments that challenge particular theodicies or their combinations. The antitheodicist argues that we ought to avoid theodicist speculation in general – or normative expectations that one ought to engage in such speculation when dealing with evil and suffering – because there is something seriously wrong, especially ethically wrong, with this speculative project itself.[19] Not only are particular theodicies (or their allegedly moderate "mere defense" versions) implausible when claiming that some X (e.g., free will or the possibility of "soul-making") is the actual or possible reason why God allows suffering; more generally, the very presupposition that *some* such justificatory or excusing reason ought to be discovered is an ethically problematic attitude to begin with in the sense of failing to sincerely acknowledge the suffering of the other in its personally experienced actual or

---

19 Admittedly, it may often be difficult to clearly distinguish between general antitheodicism and specific criticisms of theodicies (see, e.g., Wiertz 2021b, 58), but especially as we move the discussion onto a transcendental meta-level (in Chapter 5), at least one way of doing so will be indicated. For a "dissonant theodicy" claiming to recognize the irresolvability of the tension between theodicy and antitheodicy, see McLaughlin 2025a, 2025b.

possible meaninglessness. Antitheodicism encourages us to lucidly recognize the fact that, at least in some cases, it amounts to a serious ethical failure of properly responding to another's suffering to maintain that we ought to discover a reason for that suffering in terms of some justificatory meaningfulness.

According to antitheodicists, the moral failure of theodicies is at its most striking when one's theodicy is explicitly self-focused, as the case may be in soul-making theodicies, in particular. The reality of evil and suffering is justified or excused in this theodicy by the fact that both the victims and those who have a chance to help them and alleviate their sufferings can grow as human beings. The sufferings undergone or encountered may, so to speak, make their souls better. Our own selves are at the center of such a theodicy to the extent that soul-making theodicies could amount to unethical forms of "moral posing" – or so, at least, antitheodicist critics may argue. A typical moral antitheodicy is, then, an argument against a particular theodicy (e.g., the soul-making theodicy) along these or similar lines. Antitheodicism, however, is a broader normative view according to which we ought to avoid not only particular theodicies but the entire framework of theodicy.

The normative distinction between theodicism and antitheodicism can be compared to other distinctions between general views guiding or constraining the ways we examine various key issues in the philosophy of religion, such as the choice between theism and atheism or the question concerning the rationality (versus irrationality) of religious belief – even though, again, it must be kept in mind that the theodicism versus antitheodicism distinction is not restricted to the philosophy of religion. Other comparable distinctions include not only the above-mentioned one between *evidentialism* and *fideism* but also the one between *realism* and *antirealism*.[20] Just as philosophers of religion may debate not only on whether we should (or rationally may) believe in God's existence, they may debate on whether such beliefs, or other religious beliefs, ought to be supported by evidence, or rational considerations in general (evidentialism), or rather accepted or rejected independently of such considerations as matters of pure faith (fideism). While few antitheodicists embrace radical fideism, it may be suggested that there is at least a correlation (though no entailment) between antitheodicism and the criticism of evidentialism in the philosophy of religion. This is because, as already noted, to an important extent the theodicist expectation is to employ the reality of evil and suffering as an empirical premise in an essentially evidentialist debate on the rationality (versus irrationality) of theism. In contrast to continuing such typically

---

20 I examine the relations between these distinctions at some length in earlier works, especially Pihlström 2020a.

apologetic debates, as we have seen, the antitheodicist argues, on ethical grounds, that we must not instrumentalize others' suffering by subordinating it to such arguments in any way. The way in which the realism debate is related to the (anti)theodicism debate is more complex, but it can be generally suggested that antitheodicism rejects at least strong forms of *metaphysical realism* postulating a cosmic divine structure of metaphysical meaningfulness allegedly based on God's purposive scheme and an absolute perspective, a "God's-Eye View," from which those divine purposes could in principle be understood – or, again, secular versions of such metaphysical structures and perspectives, for example, teleological accounts of historical purposiveness.[21]

While it would be an exaggeration to claim that there is a necessary link between metaphysical realism and theodicism, it is important to observe that some philosophers do seem to think that realism and theodicies essentially belong together. For example, Peter Byrne (2003, vii) argues that realism[22] is needed in the philosophy of religion because responding to the problem of evil by delivering a theodicy presupposes (in his view) realism, as theism needs to incorporate a "generic offer of a theodicy" which requires a realistic conception of God conjoined with moral teleology and an account of a "final good" of human life. He maintains that the realism debate in the philosophy of religion is largely motivated by theodicism: "It is the job of religion [...] to offer human beings a theodicy" (ibid., 17). By "religion" he here means "any set of symbols (and associated actions, attitudes, feelings and experiences) providing human beings with a solution to evil by way of a theodicy" and, more generally, "that propensity in human beings (however grounded) to respond to evil by seeking the kind of meaning [...] associated with the enterprise of theodicy" (ibid., 18).

I am referring to Byrne at this length in the context of these conceptual preliminaries because he very clearly formulates an account of the interconnections between the concepts of religion, realism, and theodicy, and also explicitly attributes a search for meaning to the theodicy enterprise. In particular, realism is needed, in his view, because providing a theodicy invokes

---

21 See Pihlström 2020a, Chapter 4, for an analysis of metaphysical realism as the *proton pseudos* of theodicism. This is not to suggest that antitheodicism would necessarily be committed to antirealism, though. The realism issue is very complex, and here I cannot dwell on its details. My own view in the realism debate, both generally and in the philosophy of religion in particular, is pragmatic realism grounded in something we may call transcendental pragmatism (Pihlström 2013, 2020a, 2021, 2022, 2023).
22 Byrne (2003, 6) characterizes realism as the view according to which "the governing intent behind the concept of God is to refer to an extra-mental, extra-mundane, transcendent entity."

"a moral and providential causality in the world" transcending natural and human powers (ibid.). A realistic account of such causal structures and the ultimate human good is, for realist theodicists like Byrne, part and parcel of the project of religion as such. However, as we should not confine our theodicy versus antitheodicy discussions to the philosophy of religion, even Byrne's insistence on the close link between theodicies and realism can be extrapolated to cover secular theodicies. The common idea in all theodicies would then be, very generally expressed, that there is some ultimate way things are at the absolute metaphysical level – divinely created or not – and that whatever evils and sufferings there may be, they fall in their place at that level, receiving justification or at least an excuse when we look at the world's scheme of things from a sufficiently detached perspective (from a "God's-Eye View," as it were, no matter whether we believe in God or not). It is the availability (in principle, though presumably not in practice for us humans) of such a cosmic divine standpoint that renders suffering ultimately meaningful, even if no one except God or some imagined rational subject of historical teleology can ever grasp such meaningfulness. The antitheodicist, of course, takes a critical view on such postulations of ultimate meaning, urging us to avoid instrumentalizing suffering by subordinating it to such alleged divine purposes.

Finally, in addition to the theodicy-realism connection, it is at least equally important to pay attention to the close relation between theodicies (or theodicism) and *optimism*. Because suffering is claimed to make sense in the end, theodicies are almost by definition optimistic worldviews, and theodicism as a pursuit of theodicy typically finds optimism some kind of moral virtue. It may be taken to be courageous to continue to have faith in meaning and purpose even amid the most terrible suffering. We ought to be optimists, the theodicist would maintain, even if our current experience does not seem to warrant the claim that hardships and afflictions are ultimately meaningful. Developing theodicies and/or "defenses" is, then, a way of securing the credentials of such metaphysical or theological optimism.

Insofar as the theodicist expectation fails, however, what follows is, presumably, some form of *pessimism*, for instance atheism, according to which suffering does not make sense, after all, and there is no value or meaningfulness to be found in the world at any ultimate metaphysical level. Now, the antitheodicist can, again, ethically criticize the optimist claims of the theodicist, maintaining that it is not ethically innocent to attribute such positive value and meaningfulness to a world in which horrible things do happen, that is, that it is a way of disregarding and misrecognizing others' suffering to maintain, optimistically, that everything will ultimately turn toward the good despite the horrors that some of us have to go through. The antitheodicist may find reasons to be a pessimist – perhaps a "hopeful pessimist" (van der Lugt 2021, 2025) – but for the kind of antitheodicism I am introducing and defending in this book, the natural choice is not pessimism but *meliorism* (Lat. *melior*, better), a critical middle path between optimism and pessimism.[23] (Avoiding both optimism and pessimism in this sense can be regarded as analogous to the antitheodicist's refusing to play the apologetic game of theism versus atheism.) The meliorist antitheodicist argues that suffering is real and we ought to do whatever is within our powers to alleviate suffering and ameliorate the human condition, despite the uncertainty of the outcome. This requires taking pessimism seriously, however, and giving up the optimistic illusions of theodicies. In particular, it requires taking a critical stance to the pursuit of meaning and "meaning-making" at the heart of theodicies.

As I will argue throughout this book, particularly in Chapters 4 and 5, antitheodicism is, essentially, a *critique of meaning*. It is not a wholesale pessimistic rejection of meaningfulness but a critical stance to our naturally inevitable pursuit of meaning. As human beings living in a complex world, we can never abandon our project of finding or creating meanings in our lives, but we must realize that this is never an ethically innocent endeavor, as the very meaning-making we habitually engage in may run the risk of instrumentalizing others' sufferings in the service of the meanings we are in the business of constructing. An ethical discussion of the problems in theodicies and antitheodicism can, I hope, teach us something about the ethical complexity of living in a world in which such a search for meaning is not only inevitable but also itself a potential source of evil and suffering.

This completes our preliminary survey of the concepts needed for a critical inquiry into theodicy and antitheodicy. Our next step is a historical sketch of some of the milestones of antitheodicist thinking. Some of the arguments to be developed in later chapters have already been anticipated in the present chapter, but a more substantial articulation of antitheodicism as an ethical critique of meaning must wait until Chapters 4 and 5.

---

23 In van der Lugt's articulation of pessimism (in close relation to antitheodicy), the distinction between "future-oriented" and "value-oriented" versions of both pessimism and optimism is fundamentally important (see van der Lugt 2021, 10–13). It is value-oriented pessimism, in particular, that questions the theodicist (value-oriented) optimist view that the world, or creaturely life, is (always) valuable, despite suffering. No reference to future – as in our typically future-oriented everyday talk of optimism and pessimism – is necessary here. However, as my meliorist antitheodicism crucially utilizes pragmatism, according to which our concepts generally receive their meaning from considerations of the potential practical effects of their objects, I cannot entirely bracket the time dimension in this manner. Even value-oriented optimisms and pessimisms (and meliorism) bear some, at least implicit, reference to future expectations. (On pragmatism as a method of turning toward the future and potential future experience, see, e.g., James 1975 [1907], Lecture II.)

Chapter 3
A SKETCH OF THE HISTORY OF ANTITHEODICY

The term "antitheodicy" was coined only relatively late by Zachary Braiterman (1998, 31), who characterized antitheodicy as a religious response to the problem of evil refusing "to justify, explain, or accept as somehow meaningful the relationship between God and suffering," but the idea of antitheodicy has a considerably longer history, which may be argued to go back all the way to the *Book of Job* (see, e.g., Dahl 2019). As Mara van der Lugt (2021) shows, most of the central early modern thinkers from Pierre Bayle and Malebranche via Voltaire, Hume,[1] and Rousseau to Kant and Schopenhauer were concerned with the moral justice – or injustice – of creation, some of them advocating skepticism regarding God's existence, or even atheism, on the grounds of the problem of suffering. Leibniz's theodicy according to which the world is the best possible one was, for critics like Voltaire and Kant, the most important target. While pessimism rather than antitheodicy is at the center of van der Lugt's discussion, she joins N.N. Trakakis (2013, 2018) in characterizing antitheodicy as a primarily moral project, thus defining it more broadly than Braiterman (whose context is more explicitly theological) as "any rejection of theodicy on moral grounds" (van der Lugt 2021, 5n19). This focus on ethical reasons for rejecting theodicies is an important thread running through the history of antitheodicy, but as will be seen in later chapters (and as was already preliminarily suggested in Chapter 2), my own concept of antitheodic*ism* makes a meta-level transcendental twist by referring not as much to

---

1 As briefly noted earlier, Hume's criticism of theodicies in *Dialogues Concerning Natural Religion* (Hume 1990 [1779], chapters X-XI) is one of the central classics of philosophical literature refuting theodicies but not strictly speaking "antitheodicist" because the criticism unfolds within the argumentative game of theodicism, expecting theism to provide a theodicy and attacking it (among other things) for the reason that it fails to do so. Still, Hume did play an important role in the development of pessimism in early modern philosophy that van der Lugt (2021) examines.

straightforward moral grounds in the criticisms of theodicies but to the conditions for the possibility of having moral grounds at all.

In any event, rejecting God or defending atheism is by no means essential to antitheodicy (cf. Surin 1986). Rather, antitheodicist critique focuses on the alleged justificatory relation between God (if there is a God) and the evil and suffering there is (or, again, on secular proxies). Indeed, the most important historical figure in the emergence of antitheodicy, Kant (who, of course, did not use the term "antitheodicy"), was a Christian theist, though his Christianity is complicated and it remains debatable in what sense exactly he was committed to Christian beliefs (see, e.g., Wood 2020).

Despite Kant's significance, there were pre-Kantian formulations of antitheodicy, or at least we can interpret some of the pessimists in early modern philosophy as proto-antitheodicists. According to van der Lugt (2021, 42, 59), we may, in particular, speak of Pierre Bayle's antitheodicy (or his "'anti-theodicean' project"), especially because Bayle argued that the question of experiential pessimism is crucial not only regarding our views on God but regarding our evaluation of human existence generally. By suggesting that the history of antitheodicy really begins with Kant, I am not claiming that the pre-Kantian early modern thinkers van der Lugt (along with, e.g., Neiman 2002) discusses as pessimists questioning theodicies would not have been genuine antitheodicists. Rather, my focusing on Kantian and post-Kantian philosophy is based on my more general view on Kant as a decisive turning point in the history of philosophy – at least since antiquity – and thus, a fortiori, decisive in the theodicy discussion, too.[2] It is only from Kant onward that we can meaningfully try to formulate antitheodicism (or anything else) as an account of the necessary (transcendental) conditions for the possibility of ethics. As my transcendental philosophical methodology is fundamentally indebted to Kant, I will thus begin this historical sketch from Kant's antitheodicy and then move on to loosely "Kantian" antitheodicies and antitheodicisms.

---

2 While I have nothing against broader usages of the vocabulary of "theodicy" and "antitheodicy" that may even attribute theodicies to biblical texts (see again the essays in Laato and de Moor 2003, and on the alleged "modernity" of theodicy in particular, Sarot 2003), I do follow Neiman (2002, 2019) and van der Lugt (2021) in maintaining that only the early modern period saw the emergence of the theodicy discussion in the ethically pregnant sense we have inherited it, that is, as something in which not only some particular theological scheme but our existence as human beings sharing a world with others, and hence the comprehensibility of the world we live in, is ethically at stake. (This is neither Neiman's nor van der Lugt's formulation, though.)

3.1. Kant's Antitheodicy

Kant's 1791 essay "On the Miscarriage of All Philosophical Trials in Theodicy" is a relatively little-known piece in Kant's enormous oeuvre, at least in comparison to the three *Critiques*, but it marks a crucial step in the historical emergence of antitheodicies and antitheodicism. It is impossible to fully appreciate the significance of Kant's Theodicy Essay without a reasonably good command of his critical philosophy in general. Yet, obviously, it would be impossible to even preliminarily introduce Kant's broader philosophical project here. Suffices it to note that Kant's criticism of theodicies is an essential part of his general rejection of the idea that we could know anything whatsoever about God or transcendence. Such knowledge claims, typical in the theodicy tradition, as well as in atheists' theodicism-grounded claims to know that there is no God, violate the necessary transcendental conditions for the possibility of – and thus the inescapable boundaries of – human cognition, even though they may be naturally invited by the inevitable illusion that human reason generates when seeking metaphysical knowledge of transcendent reality.

Kant had important things to say about evil especially in Book I of his *Religionsschrift*, the 1793–94 volume titled *Religion within the Limits of Mere Reason*, in which he argued that there is "radical evil" in human nature, that is, the inextirpable inclination to prioritize maxims conflicting with the moral law. However, those discussions, as important as they are for understanding Kant's views on morality and religion and especially their mutual relations (see Wood 2020), do not explicitly address theodicies. Therefore, we will here focus on the theodicy essay, keeping in mind, however, that a full grasp of the complexities of Kant's position would require a comprehensive study of the critical philosophy. It is in the theodicy essay that Kant's antitheodicy receives its key formulation – and it is right there that the history of Western philosophy turns from theodicist assumptions to acknowledging the possibility of investigating evil and suffering ethically without such assumptions. As Richard Bernstein (2002, 4) puts it, Kant is "the modern philosopher who initiates the inquiry into evil without explicit recourse to philosophical theodicy" and hence also leads the way in our attempt to rethink the meaning of evil, suffering, and responsibility "after Auschwitz."

In opening his essay, Kant defines "theodicy" as "the defense of the highest wisdom of the creator against the charge which reason brings against it for whatever is counterpurposive [*zweckwidrig*] in the world" (8:255).[3] Theodicies

---

3 I have used the English translation of the 1791 "Theodicy Essay" available in the *Religion* volume (Kant 2018 [1793–94]); this essay, as other works by Kant, is cited in a standard manner by providing the *Akademie-Ausgabe* reference.

are expected to prove "*either* that whatever in the world we judge counterpurposive is not so; *or*, if there is any such thing, that it must be judged not at all as an intended effect but as the unavoidable consequence of the nature of things; *or*, finally, that it must at least be considered not as an intended effect of the creator of all things but, rather, merely of those beings in the world to whom something can be imputed, i.e., of human beings" (8:255). Furthermore, counterpurposiveness, in Kant's classification, can take three forms: first, the "absolutely counterpurposive, or what cannot be condoned or desired either as end or means," that is, the "morally counterpurposive," or "evil proper (sin)"; secondly, the "conditionally counterpurposive, or what can indeed never coexist with the wisdom of a will as end, yet can do so as means," that is, the "physically counterpurposive," or "ill (pain)"; and thirdly, counterpurposiveness concerning "the proportion of ill to moral evil," that is, "the disproportion between crimes and penalties in the world" (8:256–257). These varieties of counterpurposiveness challenge "the moral concept of God," that is, the creator's holiness, goodness, and justice, respectively (8:257).

It is easy to see how these versions of the counterpurposive as well as the possible theodicies that could be regarded as responses to arguments from evil (or, in Kant's terms, from counterpurposiveness) correspond to well-known theodicy debates concerning, say, the free will theodicy or the best possible world theodicy. Here we cannot explore Kant's detailed arguments against the nine different theodicies he distinguishes (8:258–263). He clearly believes to be able to refute all the arguments that have been or even could be put forward to defend God against the challenges based on counterpurposiveness. What is more interesting for our task of understanding Kant as the initiator of the antitheodicy tradition is to take a look at what happens next in the Theodicy Essay. Having refuted all attempts to vindicate God against the charges of counterpurposiveness, Kant concludes that "[e]very previous theodicy has not performed what it promised, namely the vindication of the moral wisdom of the world-government [or God] against the doubts raised against it on the basis of what the experience of this world teaches" (8:263). In order to conclude this "trial" of God and human reason, it must be considered whether "our reason is absolutely incapable of insight into *the relationship in which any world as we may ever become acquainted with through experience stands with respect to the highest wisdom*," acknowledging a "necessary limitation of what we may presume with respect to that which is too high for us" (8:263). Because we have no insight into the ground of the sensible world in the supersensible (intelligible) world, we cannot prove "the world-author's moral wisdom" (8:264).

This negative project only refutes "doctrinal" theodicies, however, that is, the kind of theodicies that, in our days, theistic analytic philosophers such as Swinburne, Plantinga, van Inwagen, or McCord Adams espouse. What remains – for Kant – to be investigated is whether an "authentic theodicy" could still be developed. By this he means "the mere dismissal of all objections against divine wisdom" as a "pronouncement of the same reason through which we form our concept of God – necessarily and prior to all experience – as a moral and wise being" (8:264). Here Kant turns to the *Book of Job*, claiming to find there an authentic interpretation of *"efficacious* practical reason," as distinguished from *"ratiocinating* (speculative) reason," allegorically expressed (8:264).[4]

The reason why we may consider Kant's "authentic theodicy" an antitheodicy is that it is a *dismissal* of objections against God – and thus, by extension, a dismissal of the theodicy arguments presented as responses to such objections. It is not a move in the argumentative game of theodicy; all those moves are, for various reasons, rejected by Kant in the first (negative) part of the Theodicy Essay. It is, instead, a proposal to change the game itself by dismissing the premises that generate the game.

From Kant's perspective, the crucial virtue exemplified by Job's character is not as much patience (emphasized in the Christian tradition, in particular) as honesty, sincerity, or truthfulness. When Job's friends come to console him, presenting various – in our terms, theodicist – reasons why his suffering might be justified or understandable, after all, Job simply refuses to accept any of those reasons. He never admits that he sinned and that therefore his sufferings would be legitimate. He continues to accuse God of injustice, of letting innocents suffer. Moreover, when God finally speaks to Job, he basically introduces the overwhelming majesty of his creation and thus his own cosmic power; certainly he does not respond to the demands of justice voiced by Job. God does say that Job has spoken rightly, unlike the friends, and thus the sympathy of the author(s) of the book seems to be on the side of the honest sufferer. It is right here that Kant praises Job's moral virtue:

> Job speaks as he thinks, and with the courage with which he, as well as every human being in his position, can well afford; his friends, on the contrary, speak as if they were being secretly listened to by the mighty one, over whose cause they are passing judgment, and as if gaining his

---

4 On the significance of the *Book of Job* for philosophical criticisms of theodicies generally, see Dahl 2019; cf. Newsom 2019. It must also be admitted that there are various elements of theodicy, or even theodicies, at work in *The Book of Job* (see Illman 2003), a book full of internal tensions, and thus the Kantian treatment of Job's suffering here is not primarily intended as an interpretation of the biblical text itself. According to Neiman (2019, 365), Kant was the first philosopher to openly sympathize with Job.

favor through their judgment were closer to their heart than the truth. Their malice in pretending to assert things into which they yet must admit they have no insight, and in simulating a conviction which they in fact do not have, contrasts with Job's frankness [...]. (8:265–266)

This "frankness" (*Freimütigkeit*) is grounded in Job's "sincerity of heart" (*Aufrichtigkeit des Herzens*)[5] and "honesty in openly admitting one's doubts" (*die Redlichkeit, seine Zweifel unverhohlen zu gestehen*), establishing "the preeminence of the honest man over the religious flatterer [*Schmeichler*] in the divine verdict" (8:267). Accordingly, for Kant, the central Joban virtues are "sincerity in taking notice of the impotence of our reason" and "honesty in not distorting our thoughts in what we say, however pious our intention" (8:267). Sincerity is "the principal requirement in matters of faith," and while we could always be mistaken in what we believe or claim to know, we can and ought to "stand by the *truthfulness* [*Wahrhaftigkeit*]" of what we say (8:267).[6]

Given the significance of these Joban virtues in Kant's discussion, it can even be argued that theodicism – represented by Job's friends, heavily criticized as insincere flatterers by Kant – amounts to dishonesty. Theodicies are, in a sense, lies, specifically lies to oneself (see 8:268–269). Admittedly, the friends are not liars in the sense that they would deliberately say something they know to be false. However, the friends are mere literary figures used by the biblical author – and Kant as a philosophical interpreter – as exemplifications of the moral viciousness of theodicy. Moreover, the Kantian critique of theodicies should, I submit, primarily be understood as a self-criticism, placed within the general reflexive critique of reason in the critical philosophy. As will be emphasized in later chapters, the ethical seriousness of antitheodicism is manifested in its self-critical orientation: we should actively identify situations in which we are tempted to think like Job's friends, explicitly or implicitly finding meaning and purpose in others' suffering, and should seek to liberate ourselves from such habits of thought.

Not only do theodicies fail, according to Kant, in justifying evil and suffering. Kant maintains that there is a sense in which they are themselves evil.[7]

---

5 It is noteworthy that Kant speaks of the sincerity of *heart*. This readily compares to the importance attached to the "change of heart" (*Herzensänderung*) from radical evil to moral virtue in Book I of the *Religionsschrift*. For an important discussion (not referring to theodicy), see Wood 2020, Chapter 4.
6 For an excellent discussion of Kant's account of sincerity and integrity in the Theodicy Essay, see van der Lugt 2021, 313–317; see also Neiman 2019, 366–367.
7 For a somewhat comparable non-Kantian argument, see Tilley's (1991) speech-act-theoretical analysis of theodicies as evil.

Distorting our "inner declarations" before our own conscience is "*in itself* evil even if it harms no one" (8:270). Accordingly, Kant seems to say in so many words that theodicies are exemplifications of evil. They are, moreover, evil in a distinctive sense, failing to acknowledge the Enlightenment ideal of free, autonomous, and sincere thinking. They are, then, revolts against humanity (as conceived of in a Kantian way): the kind of insincerity at work in theodicies is a failure to recognize the very core of Kantian autonomy, freedom and responsibility in thinking. Therefore, the "authentic theodicy" incorporating the idea of sincerity is, actually, an antitheodicy. What Kant is telling us, on my reading, is that theodicies are not only evil but, arguably, in his specific sense "radically evil" (taking the etymology of *radix*, root, seriously): an inclination to theodicist thinking is deeply, perhaps inextricably, rooted in us, especially in our temptation to prioritize our own peace of mind and our need to see the world as a smoothly functioning harmonious system, instead of honestly seeing the disharmony and ugliness of what there is, in comparison to our ethical duty to avoid instrumentalizing others in the service of such illusory hope for harmony. Thus, we tend to engage in "meaning-making" that allegedly renders human suffering meaningful even if we know, or at least ought to know, fully well that such meaning may be an illusion – perhaps a humanly inescapable "transcendental illusion,"[8] but an illusion nevertheless.[9]

---

8 I am not claiming that Kant would believe that the illusoriness of theodicies is of the kind we find in what he calls transcendental illusion (see the Transcendental Dialectic of the *First Critique*). This is merely an analogy, but an illuminating one, I think.

9 A lot more could and should be said about Kant's relation to theodicies and theodicism. Mara van der Lugt (2021, 317n94) is presumably right to point out that Kant is not, at least not clearly, an antitheodicist, given his attempt to defend an authentic theodicy. While influential readers of Kant (e.g., Bernstein 2002; Neiman 2002) in my view rightly portray Kant as the first philosopher to think about the problem of evil and suffering without recourse to theodicy, others take the ideas of "authentic theodicy" and a "theodicy of protest" more seriously and offer what remain at least semi-theodicist readings of Kant (see, e.g., Roth 2001; Brachtendorff 2002; Galbraith 2006). Whatever the final truth about Kant's own views is (and we are not pursuing such truth here), Neiman is in my view correct in emphasizing – reaching toward a transcendental antitheodicism, without using that term – that according to Kant theodicies, and specifically claims to know the connections between moral and natural evils, would "undermine the possibility of morality" and that therefore "solving" the problem of evil would be immoral, tending toward blasphemy (Neiman 2002, 69). Of course, for a Kantian, it is more important that theodicies are immoral (or even evil) than that they are blasphemous (if they are), but the close relation between these moral and religious vices again highlights the fact that antitheodicism, especially in the Kantian tradition, need not be non- or anti-religious (though of course it can be). Whatever theological vices theodicies are guilty of, the more fundamental vice is moral. However, more

Later antitheodicist views are broadly speaking Kantian in their attempts to uncover the illusory and essentially dishonest character of theodicies (as well as, in some cases at least, in their implicitly transcendental orientation). This is the case even if they are in no other way "Kantian," that is, even if their authors (like William James) rejected most of the essential points of Kant's thought.

3.2. "Kantian" Antitheodicy: Schopenhauer and Beyond

In addition to locating the sources of antitheodicist thinking in Kant's "Theodicy Essay," we may, then, loosely speak of "Kantian" antitheodicy as something that emerges, explicitly or implicitly, from Kant's ideas while not following Kant's own moral or theological views in any detail.

One of the most important post-Kantian philosophers arriving at what we today may call antitheodicy was, of course, Arthur Schopenhauer. In a key passage in his main work, *Die Welt als Wille und Vorstellung*, he wrote:

> What is more, in fact, we very soon look upon the world as something whose non-existence is not only conceivable, but even preferable to its existence. Therefore our astonishment at it easily passes into a brooding over that *fatality* which could nevertheless bring about its existence, and by virtue of which such an immense force as is demanded for the production and maintenance of such a world could be directed so much against its own interest and advantage. Accordingly, philosophical astonishment is at bottom one that is dismayed and distressed; philosophy, like the overture to *Don Juan*, starts with a minor chord. (Schopenhauer 1969 [1819, 1844], vol. II, 171; original emphasis.)

According to Schopenhauer, then, our fundamental philosophical urge "springs from the sight of the *evil and wickedness* in the world" (ibid.; original emphasis). This reminds us that Schopenhauer's pessimism, though developed as a system of Kant-inspired idealistic metaphysics, contains an empirical element: it is the "sight" of wickedness that leads us to philosophize about the world and our place in it. As Schopenhauer concludes: "Not merely that the world exists, but still more that it is such a miserable and melancholy world, is the *punctum pruriens* of metaphysics, the problem awakening in mankind an unrest that cannot be quieted either by scepticism or criticism" (ibid. 172).

---

depth will be added to these considerations by taking a properly transcendental turn in subsequent chapters.

Schopenhauer famously argued against Leibniz that we live in the *worst* – certainly not the best – possible world (see Schopenhauer 1969 [1819, 1844], vol. I, Book IV, §59 [323-326], and vol. II, §46 [573-588]), concluding that optimism, if it is not simple thoughtlessness, is "not merely an absurd, but also a really *wicked*, way of thinking, a bitter mockery of the unspeakable suffering of mankind" (ibid., vol. I, 326).[10] This reads like an early statement of the essentially ethical rejection of theodicies we are familiar with after twentieth-century horrors such as the Holocaust. For straightforwardly ethical reasons, philosophy must not resort to such optimism. Schopenhauer's pessimism, even if too extreme for many of us, may be regarded as a starting point for a moral critique of theodicism questioning the optimist's (or the theodicist's) ability to adequately acknowledge the reality of suffering. In another oft-cited passage, Schopenhauer wrote in 1819:

> If we were to conduct the most hardened and callous optimist through hospitals, infirmaries, operating theatres, through prisons, torture-chambers, and slave-hovels, over battlefields and to places of execution; if we were to open to him all the dark abodes of misery, where it shuns the gaze of old curiosity, and finally were to allow him to glance into the dungeon of Ugolino where prisoners are starved to death, he too would certainly see in the end what kind of a world is this *meilleur des mondes possibles*. (Ibid., vol. I, 325)

In the 1844 second volume of his *magnum opus*, he continues: 'Actually optimism cuts so strange a figure on this scene of sin, suffering, and death, that we should be forced to regard it as irony if we did not have an adequate explanation of its origin in its secret source (namely hypocritical flattery with an offensive confidence in its success)" (ibid., vol. II, 583). Like Kant, Schopenhauer thus characterizes optimism (and thus, analogously, theodicy) as dishonest flattery.

Schopenhauer's pessimist antitheodicy (if we may call it that) is also "Kantian" in the sense that Schopenhauer was directly influenced by Kant's transcendental philosophy. In contrast, the more recent historical antitheodicies to be briefly introduced in the rest of this chapter are in my view "Kantian" in the broader sense of investigating antitheodicy as a necessary condition for the possibility of an ethical understanding of suffering. This does not mean that any of their authors would be "Kantian" in the specific

---

10 As Neiman (2019, 377) puts it, much of Schopenhauer's work can actually be seen as "anti-*Theodicy*," an explicit rejection of the book by Leibniz which "Schopenhauer so loathed as to say its only merit was to inspire 'the immortal *Candide*' ".

sense of endorsing, say, his conception of ethics. They may not explicitly refer to Kant at all, and they might even strongly disagree with any attribution of "Kantian" ways of thinking to them. The phrase "Kantian antitheodicy" should thus be understood with reference to the basic Kantian, or at least Kant-inspired, idea of critical or transcendental investigation (preliminarily introduced in the previous chapter and to be revisited in Chapter 5). Antitheodicy, in my loosely Kantian framework, is claimed to be constitutive of a genuinely ethical stance on evil and suffering, or even of moral seriousness as such. Theodicies are not merely contingently wrong answers to the problem of evil and suffering – answers that could be right but for some reason fail. Instead, they are profoundly misguided in their very point of departure. Antitheodicy is, in this Kantian vein, claimed to be necessary for our being able to make sense of our ethical predicament, analogously to the way in which Kant's transcendental conditions for the possibility of cognitive experience (e.g., space and time, or the categories) are claimed to be necessary and constitutive.

However, it may be too straightforward to classify Schopenhauer as an antitheodicist simply because of his self-evident standing as the greatest pessimist in the history of philosophy. As van der Lugt (2021, 370) interestingly explains, there is a sense in which Schopenhauer follows a theodicist logic, after all – albeit a secular one, because he does not find suffering justifiable in terms of any divine reasons. Suffering involves guilt based on our mere existence (ibid., 366), and therefore it is not simply "pointless"; moreover, there is a "way out" of suffering, and therefore Schopenhauer, in van der Lugt's view, ends up with a paradoxical "pessimist theodicy" (ibid., 370–371). Schopenhauer is thus difficult to classify in the terms of our discussion.

3.3. Pragmatist Antitheodicy

While pragmatist philosophers are sometimes taken to be naïve optimists believing in our human capacities of constructing meanings in the world we live in and transform by means of our action, this popular conception is highly misleading. William James, one of the two co-founders of pragmatism (along with Charles S. Peirce), explicitly proposed meliorism as a middle ground between optimism and pessimism (see Chapter 2), and his rejection of theodicies is an important step in the development of antitheodicism, although he did not use that term any more than Kant or other earlier classics did.

It may nevertheless seem prima facie odd to deal with pragmatism in this context. Pragmatism might be taken to be a form of instrumentalism or (in ethics) utilitarianism, or at least consequentialism, easily sliding into (secular) theodicies excusing evil and suffering by invoking the actual or potential beneficial effects for which sufferings would be a "price" to be paid. Wouldn't the pragmatist be the first to maintain that "aims justify means"? Indeed, pragmatism might even seem to be a philosophy not taking evil and suffering sufficiently seriously. This, however, is a vulgar picture of pragmatism. While some classical and modern pragmatists, including, perhaps, most prominently John Dewey, may have been too limited in their acknowledgment of the reality of evil and the tragic dimensions of human life and history, this is certainly not the case with James, who was preoccupied with the problem of evil through his entire life.

While James was no Kantian,[11] the Kantian position emphasizing individual sincerity we encountered in Section 3.1 above also seems to come close to James's view: there is something fundamentally *insincere* in theodicies and more generally in the optimist way of viewing the world failing to take the reality of suffering seriously.[12] James implicitly follows not so much Kant but the arch-pessimist Schopenhauer when maintaining in the opening lecture of *Pragmatism* that optimist philosophers "are dealing in shades, while those who live and feel know truth" (James 1975 [1907], 22): in particular, a Leibnizian theodicy with its "best possible world," postulating an ultimately harmonious universe, is "a cold literary exercise, whose cheerful substance even hell-fire does not warm" (ibid., 20). It is fundamentally this same problem that troubles "all rationalistic systems" that are plagued by "unreality" and remain "out of touch with concrete facts of joys and sorrows" (ibid., 17) – that is, out of touch with the reality of suffering. Schopenhauer could easily have joined James in describing Leibniz by saying that "no realistic image of the experience of a damned soul had ever approached the portals of his mind" (ibid., 20). James no less than Schopenhauer was thus diametrically opposed to "the airy and shallow optimism of current religious philosophy" (ibid.), reminding us that evil and suffering, far from being mere shadows of the perfection of absolute reality, are fully real in their own right, "the condition of the only beings known to us anywhere in the universe with a developed consciousness of what the universe is" (ibid., 21).[13] The optimist and the theodicist are not

---

11 However, I have argued on a number of occasions that there are important Kantian elements in James's overall philosophical project; see, e.g., Pihlström 2021, Chapter 3.
12 On sincerity as a major theme in the critique of theodicy, especially in Kant's antitheodicism, see again van der Lugt 2021, 315–317; and Kivistö and Pihlström 2016, Chapter 2 (see also Section 3.1). On James's appreciation of Schopenhauer's "honesty," see Leary 2015, 12.
13 See also, in particular, the discussion of the "sick soul" in *The Varieties of Religious Experience*: according to James (1958 [1902], 137–139), the sick soul is someone who temperamentally views the "evil facts" of the world as "the best key to life's

just naïve but get *everything* wrong; their entire way of viewing the world is ethically misguided. Thus, while the antitheodicist argument starts from an empirical – or, as we might also say, phenomenological – description of the concrete experiential manifestations of suffering in our world, the true significance of this argument is transcendental, pertaining to the constitutive conditions of our ability to think about the world in general; accordingly, what we have here is a case of pragmatically naturalized transcendental reflection (though, again, such terms were of course not used by James).

Given James's antipathy to Kantian transcendental philosophy, it may seem strange to introduce his antitheodicy as a reaction to Kant's and Schopenhauer's antitheodicies. However, it can be argued that James, as much as Kant, engages in antitheodicy by suggesting that we ought to view evil and suffering from the standpoint of ethics (practical reason) instead of metaphysics. Moreover, he follows Schopenhauer in taking the pessimistic challenge seriously: we have a clear ethical need to avoid excessive optimism that fails to take the reality of suffering for what it is. As against the illusions of optimism and theodicy, what James proposes is meliorism rather than Schopenhauerian pessimism, however.

The above-quoted antitheodicist phrases attacking Leibnizian and Hegelian theodicies occur in the first lecture of James's *Pragmatism*. The 1907 book both opens and closes with the problem of evil, and therefore it can be suggested that an antitheodicist approach to this problem provides a frame within which James introduces his pragmatism and the many applications of the pragmatic method he develops regarding, for example, metaphysics and the concept of truth. One of the best-known formulations of meliorism can be found toward the end of *Pragmatism*, where James contrasts it with both optimism and pessimism:

> We all do wish to minimize the insecurity of the universe; we are and ought to be unhappy when we regard it as exposed to every enemy and open to every life-destroying draft. Nevertheless there are unhappy men who think the salvation of the world impossible. Theirs is the doctrine known as pessimism.

---

significance, and possibly the only openers of our eyes to the deepest levels of truth," admits that they are "as genuine parts of nature as the good ones," and even maintains that "[t]he completest religions would therefore seem to be those in which the pessimistic elements are best developed." The significance of this Jamesian view for "hopeful pessimism" is also recognized by van der Lugt (2021, 415). Roth (2004, 292) observes, with reference to James: "Shadowed by the Holocaust and other genocides, ours is a time for sick souls."

Optimism in turn would be the doctrine that thinks the world's salvation inevitable.

Midway between the two there stands what may be called the doctrine of meliorism, tho it has hitherto figured less as a doctrine than as an attitude in human affairs. Optimism has always been the regnant *doctrine* in european [sic] philosophy. Pessimism was only recently introduced by Schopenhauer and counts few systematic defenders as yet. (Ibid., 137; original emphasis)

It is crucial to acknowledge the seriousness with which James took Schopenhauerian pessimism. The antitheodicist message of *Pragmatism* (and other works by James) becomes clearer when he observes that the very idea of meliorism – as the active pragmatic commitment to making the world better – is grounded in a kind of pessimism that finds evil, suffering, insecurity, and loss real elements of the world we live in, instead of claiming them to be merely apparent in the style of optimist theodicies. Thus, James continues:

In particular *this* query has always come home to me: May not the claims of tender-mindedness go too far? May not the notion of a world already saved *in toto* anyhow, be too saccharine to stand? May not religious optimism be too idyllic? Must *all* be saved? Is *no* price to be paid in the work of salvation? Is the last word sweet? Is all "yes, yes" in the universe? Doesn't the fact of "no" stand at the very core of life? Doesn't the very "seriousness" that we attribute to life mean that ineluctable noes and losses form a part of it, that there are genuine sacrifices somewhere, and that something permanently drastic and bitter always remains at the bottom of its cup?

I cannot speak officially as a pragmatist here; all I can say is that my own pragmatism offers no objection to my taking sides with this more moralistic view, and giving up the claim of total reconciliation. [...] It is then perfectly possible to accept sincerely a drastic kind of a universe from which the element of 'seriousness' is not to be expelled. Whoso does so is, it seems to me, a genuine pragmatist. (Ibid., 141–142.)

This is a key idea in antitheodicist thinking in general: we should be wary of claims of "total reconciliation," acknowledging the reality of irrecoverable losses and sufferings, but this should not prevent us from doing whatever we can to ameliorate the bleak human condition. Jamesian pragmatism reminds us that antitheodicism, even though it frames our serious philosophical project in general (and not merely our specific engagement in the problem of evil or in the philosophy of religion), is not doomed to cynical nihilism but should be regarded as a constitutive condition for our active engagement in rendering the world better. In these ameliorating efforts, we should, borrowing apt phrases from James's other works, do our best to get rid of our "instinctive blindness" to other human beings' experiences and to avoid being deaf to the "cries of the wounded."[14] Meliorism acknowledges real loss.

Furthermore, one of the lessons of pragmatist antitheodicy is the impossibility of approaching the problem of evil and suffering by assuming a dichotomy between theory and practice. When we understand the problem of evil as a frame for the development of not only pragmatism but philosophy in general (as, I think, we should do when appreciating James's *Pragmatism*), our philosophical orientation as such depends on a way of viewing the world already informed by an antitheodicist seriousness regarding meaningless suffering as something we must attend to in investigating what it even means to rationally apply concepts to the world we live in. Insofar as we acknowledge, abandoning the theodicy project, the full reality of suffering in its (potential) purposelessness and absurdity, nothing in our relation to the world and to other human beings will remain the same anymore. When we take this idea seriously, realizing that we cannot divorce our antitheodicism from our way of viewing the world in general, we can no longer distinguish between responding to suffering theoretically and responding to it practically. There is no conceptual space for such a dichotomy. The very attempt to speculatively theorize at a purely metaphysical or epistemological level about theodicies (or "defenses") is itself a failure of acknowledging others' pain.

This also leads us to appreciate the significance of antitheodic*ism* as a general approach – or a way of viewing the world – rather than particular antitheodicies as direct challenges to particular theodicies. Antitheodicism, developed along pragmatist lines, seeks to evaluate the ethical standing of our world-engagement, that is, our practices of thinking about and dealing with suffering. It cautions us against easy appeals to justifications or excuses, while fully realizing that our practices are full of attempts at such justifications and excuses. Accordingly, a pragmatist antitheodicy, especially when conjoined with a Jamesian pragmatist understanding of the meaning of truth in terms of pragmatic truthfulness normatively constraining our practices of pursuing the truth (cf. ibid., Lecture VI), conceived of as an ethical virtue ultimately indistinguishable from antitheodicism (see also Pihlström 2021), is a continuous criticism of the temptations to dishonesty and insincerity – untruthfulness – that

---

14 For the blindness metaphor, see the lecture "On a Certain Blindness in Human Beings," in James 1962 [1899], and for the "cries of the wounded," see the essay "The Moral Philosopher and the Moral Life," in James 1979 [1897]. I discuss both at some length in my many publications on James's pragmatism, including Pihlström 2020a.

plague our practices of responding to suffering and could ruin any of our practices of inquiry and world-engagement.[15]

3.4. Wittgensteinian Antitheodicy

A loosely identifiable tradition known as "Wittgensteinian" moral philosophy and philosophy of religion emerged during the second half of the twentieth century, associated with Ludwig Wittgenstein's early followers and interpreters such as Rush Rhees and Norman Malcolm, as well as their students, including Peter Winch and D.Z. Phillips, and several later Wittgenstein-inspired thinkers, such as Raimond Gaita and Andrew Gleeson.[16] While Wittgenstein himself had very little to say (directly) on the problem of evil and suffering – and the little he did say was not "antitheodicist" at all, because especially in his early philosophy he tended to think of ethics as an ineffable contemplation of the world *sub specie aeternitatis* (from the perspective of eternity), rather than from a finite human perspective – many of the so-called Wittgensteinians have defended antitheodicist approaches, primarily taking their departure from late-Wittgensteinian reflections on religious language-use that emphasize its differences to (for example) scientific, theoretical, and explanatory ways of speaking.[17] This is presumably most obvious in Phillips's work.

---

15 Interpreting James as an antitheodicist is compatible with recognizing that the pragmatist tradition – a heterogeneous tradition full of many tensions – may also contain theodicist elements. See, e.g., Cornel West's (1989) development of what he calls "prophetic pragmatism" as an "American theodicy" (ibid., 6), specifically an "Emersonian theodicy" yielding a culture of creative democracy that nevertheless acknowledges the reality of evil and the tragic.
16 While Phillips is by far the best-known and most influential antitheodicist among these philosophers (and therefore the main character of this section), Gleeson (2012) also explicitly criticizes theodicist approaches to the problem of evil, proposing a rethinking of divine love along antitheodicist lines.
17 I won't discuss Wittgenstein's own views directly in this section (or this book). Let me just note that I am one of those who prefer to approach Wittgenstein from a Kantian angle, emphasizing his focus – early and late – on the (historically mutable and reinterpretable) conditions for the possibility of linguistic meaning and/or communication as well as the limits of language based thereupon (see, e.g., Appelqvist 2020). This is not unrelated to the (anti)theodicy issue, because it turns out that leading Wittgensteinians, including Phillips, typically argue that theodicies are violations of religious and ethical language-use. Accordingly, while Wittgenstein's own views are not our concern here, a typical argumentative strategy in the Wittgensteinian framework draws attention to the ways in which theodicies can be seen as misuses of language, ultimately verging on absurdity.

This is not to claim that Wittgenstein himself would not have had a deep interest in the significance of suffering. Just consider, for instance, the central role played by examples of pain language in his discussions of the meaning of psychological language-use, especially in the so-called Part II of the *Philosophical Investigations*, where we find the famous remark about my having an "attitude towards a soul" toward another person in pain, without this entailing that I would have the "opinion" (*Meinung*) that he "has" a soul (Wittgenstein 1953, Part II, iv) – or that it would be an epistemological problem (prior to my ethical attitude to him) to ascertain whether he does. Or consider this quotation from *Culture and Value*:

> Life can educate you to "believing in God". And *experiences* too are what do this but not visions, or other sense experiences, which show us the "existence of this being", but e.g. sufferings of various sorts. And they do not show us God as a sense experience does an object, nor do they give rise to *conjectures* about him. Experiences, thoughts – life can force this concept on us. (Wittgenstein 1998 [1980], 86; original emphases.)

When life "educates" us into a certain view (religious or not) about the meaning or meaninglessness of suffering, for instance, then philosophical rationalizations offered from a vantage point external to that life are of only very limited use. Theodicies, with no organic relation to real lives of suffering, may thus even verge on nonsensicality.

Wittgensteinian philosophers, hence, typically question not the truth but the *sense* of theodicies attributing reasonable and moral purposes to God in relation to suffering.[18] According to Stephen Mulhall (1994, 18), for example, God's motivations would themselves be evil if, say, the starving of a child played a role in his allegedly good overall plan. It is not only ethically problematic but, in the religious context, superstitious or blasphemous to offer an apology defending God's plan in such cases. That is, it is both ethically and religiously wrong to set up ethical criteria for God; moreover, such an endeavor is conceptually misguided and ultimately without sense. This is because if we primarily approach the problem of evil purely intellectually, as a theoretical puzzle, we can hardly avoid ending up with a picture of God as an "evil demon," which makes little sense. "Such a justification of the ways

---

18 Indeed, from a Wittgensteinian perspective, it is natural to wonder what it could even mean to claim a theodicy to be "true" (or false, for that matter). What is at issue is not whether theodicies get some worldly – or divine – facts right but whether they make sense at all as human responses to reality.

of God to man[19] amounts to little less than blasphemy," Mulhall concludes (ibid., 19).

Similarly, the entanglement of the ethical and the conceptual in antitheodicy is emphasized by Andrew Gleeson (2012, Chapter 1), who maintains that the very concept of morality would collapse if we subscribed to theodicist "bargains" by viewing human suffering, particularly innocent children's suffering, as a possibly legitimate price that could be paid for some overall good – even if that good concerned the victims themselves. While suffering may sometimes be beneficial (even to the victim), this can never be used to morally justify the reality of suffering, or to justify, in the theistic context, God's having created a world with suffering; such a bargain would turn both God and humans into monsters and should be viewed with horror (ibid., 4, 11–14). Indeed, horror would be the only appropriate response to someone who really suggested that being murdered in a gas chamber could possibly be something that a victim – even an innocent child – could ultimately be reconciled with in a beatific harmony in the hereafter. For Wittgenstein-inspired thinkers like Mulhall and Gleeson, theodicies are profoundly confused violations of the constitutive criteria of a religious attitude to life and the world, breaching the rules of religious (and ethical) language-use. A comparison to Kantian critical philosophy invites itself (despite the Wittgensteinians' overall non-Kantianism): just as for Kant theodicies illegitimately transgress the boundaries of human cognition, in the Wittgensteinian context they transgress the bounds of sense.

One of the key debates on theodicy versus antitheodicy in the recent history of the philosophy of religion took place in the 1970s between Phillips and one of the leading representatives of evidentialist analytic philosophy of religion, Richard Swinburne. It is therefore natural to formulate a Phillipsian-Wittgensteinian antitheodicy in critical response to a Swinburnean theodicy, and of course, by extension, to other evidentialist or rationalizing theodicies of the same kind.[20] In his early debate with Phillips, Swinburne (1977, 99) – in line with the theodicies at work in mainstream analytic philosophy of religion even today – stated that "it is a good thing that a creator should make a half-finished universe and create immature creatures, who are humanly free agents, to inhabit it," as those immature creatures may then also grow

---

19 The phrase "justify the ways of God to man" is drawn from Milton's *Paradise Lost*, which in its poetic way explains the fall of Satan and thus the origin of evil. Milton's epic is analyzed as a "literary theodicy" in Danielsson 1982; on Milton and (anti)theodicy, see also Clement 2020.
20 See Phillips 2004 for what is presumably his main work on the problem of evil, summarizing his criticism of theodicies. For a clarifying overview, see Koistinen 2022.

spiritually as they encounter suffering and evil. Ultimately all is well in God's overall plan, and even though our human capacities are limited, we can understand that this plan is good.

As against views like this, Phillips (along with other Wittgensteinian antitheodicists) argues that what Swinburne offers us is not genuine freedom and responsibility but a vulgar "pseudoresponsibility" (Phillips 1977, 110). Instead of justifying or excusing God's ways with reference to God's having created us as free and responsible, we should perceive that any purportedly "higher" reasons that God might be taken to have for allowing suffering, including the need to maintain human beings' moral responsibility based on their freedom, are unavailable to us, as we lack any transcendent perspective. However, more importantly, if there were such a "'higher' form of reasoning among God and his angels," then "so much the worse for God and his angels" (ibid., 116). If there were a justification for the Holocaust, for instance, "that would make it all the more monstrous" (Phillips 1991, 198; see also Phillips 2005).[21] Instead of pursuing such pseudo-justifications, the religious believer in Phillips's sense finds us living in "a world where disasters of natural and moral kinds can strike without rhyme or reason" and is thus unable to accept the theodicist picture of "order, optimism, and progress" (Phillips 1977, 119). There is, then, a crude moral insensitivity in theodicies (ibid., 118), rendering them superstitious or even blasphemous due to their inherent inability to recognize the impossibility of all-encompassing harmony or reconciliation in our messy human world of finitude, contingency, and vulnerability. It is particularly insensitive to refer to sufferings as opportunities for moral growth – along the lines of, for example, Swinburne (1998, 68) – as it is nothing less than absurd to conceptualize, say, the horrors of the Holocaust along such lines (see Phillips 2004, 59; Koistinen 2022, §5). Again, the absurdity at work here is both conceptual and ethical (as well as, possibly, religious).

Phillips's criticism of Swinburne and other theodicists is grounded in his general rejection of "rationalist" and speculative theoretical approaches in the philosophy of religion. What this means, among other things, is that Phillips challenges not only theistic theodicies (such as Swinburne's) but also the atheist arguments sharing the same presuppositions (see Koistinen 2022). As another Wittgensteinian puts it, the problem of evil "is not theoretical,

---

21 For an illuminating discussion of Phillips's argument in this regard, see Burley 2012a, 147–148. Schönbaumsfeld (2018, 103), also discussing Phillips, says that the assumption creating the horrendousness and confusions of theodicy is the idea that "God is a member of our moral community, and a calculating consequentialist at that"; rejecting that assumption, we realize that "theodicies already fall at the first hurdle."

but is the practical problem of how one lives a religious life in a world of evil and misfortune, a life that includes, among other things, worship, prayer, and faith in God" (Tilghman 1994, 114). Similarly, Mikel Burley (commenting on Phillips's and Wittgenstein's views) speaks of the "inadequacy of any merely theoretical response to pain and suffering," suggesting that the theodicist is "so confused as to be unaware of the degree of their own insensitivity" (Burley 2012b, §5).[22] No appeal to the possibility of a rational divine order behind the world of suffering – along Swinburne's or other theodicists' lines – is considered sufficient or even relevant as a response to such a fundamental challenge to epistemology-centered ways of approaching the problem. Theodicies, seeking a systematic divine world-order and failing to recognize the precariousness of life, "have the immoral audacity to try to impose a false order on life's contingencies" (Phillips 1993, 162), whereas the truly religious believer does not even try to "tidy up" the messy reality we live in (ibid., 166–168). For the latter, it is literally nonsensical to claim to come up with, say, ethical rules that God ought to obey and within which God's creation, including suffering, must be kept.

The Wittgensteinian paradigm in antitheodicism is, accordingly, characterized by a thoroughly ethical orientation to the problem of evil and suffering. It is an ethical task for us to learn to view reality without illusions of harmony. In particular, there is something deeply morally offensive in "self-regarding" theodicies such as the soul-making theodicy. Toby Betenson (2016, 61), citing Phillips's antitheodicy formulations, notes that committing a moral action purely for self-regarding reasons aiming at the development of one's own character seriously harms the moral value of the action. According to both Phillips (2004) and Betenson (2016, 61), soul-making theodicies, in particular, view others' sufferings as opportunities *for me* "to be shown at my best," but when we approach others' sufferings in this manner, we will ironically be shown at our worst. The beautiful "selfie" of the morally laudable subject is corrupted into something like the picture of Dorian Gray in Oscar Wilde's famous novel.[23]

Hence, a central shortcoming in the entire theodicy paradigm, according to the Wittgensteinians (as well as the pragmatists, as we saw), is its tendency to overintellectualize philosophy of religion and philosophy, including ethics,

---

22 Burley (2012b, §5) argues that Phillips himself is confused, too, aiming at a detached perspective of contemplative philosophy also risking a certain kind of indifference to suffering. For a sympathetic analysis of Phillips's conception of contemplative philosophy, see Koistinen 2011.

23 On theodicies and the "moral selfie culture" of our times, see Pihlström and Kivistö 2023, Chapter 2.

more generally. As Phillips repeatedly emphasizes, the aim of the philosophy of religion, as practiced along Wittgenstein-inspired lines, is neither to defend nor to criticize any religious outlook but to understand critically the meanings of the language-use at issue and to analyze and overcome possible misuses of language, such as theodicies. Instead of overintellectualization, religious belief should be seen as a potential natural response by some, but not all, to the problems of life, including suffering. Hence, the Wittgensteinians would be among the first to insist that antitheodicy does not amount to atheism, even though it might initially seem so; on the contrary, theodicies share with atheist arguments from evil the tendency to breach the constitutive rules of religious language-use.

Accordingly, the possible value of religious responses to life should not be vulgarized, according to Phillips and other Wittgensteinians, by stretching the meanings of words such as "justification" and "evil" beyond their legitimate uses in the language-games that religious individuals engage in. Nor should any metaphysical or theological explanations of evil (as distinguished from ordinary scientific, psychological, or social ones, for instance) be offered to allegedly render evil more "meaningful." The problem, in Wittgensteinian terms, in explaining why God allows suffering is not that theodicies formulating such explanations are bad explanations but that they are explanations in the first place. Even an attempt at a justificatory explanation of suffering is a misunderstanding of religious concepts and their place in our lives. Suffering may be, and often is, a serious problem for a religious believer *within* their religious lives, but it is a misconstrual to view it as an epistemic challenge to that life – or its alleged metaphysical commitments – from the outside, so to speak. Therefore, atheist arguments from evil, relying on the reality of suffering as an empirical premise providing evidence against God's existence (see Chapter 2), are equally misguided and conceptually confused as theists' theodicies. The problem of evil and suffering *cannot* meaningfully function as an atheist argument any more than its proper responses can theoretically justify God's reasons for allowing suffering.

One of the most important lessons to take home from Wittgensteinian antitheodicy is, then, the entanglement of the conceptual and the ethical confusions of theodicism.[24] According to Phillips (1993, 157), "Job cannot make *sense* of his afflictions in terms of [theodicist] arguments of his would-be comforters." Whereas theodicists (at least implicitly if not explicitly) calculate what

---

24 For this reason, I am not convinced by views sharply distinguishing between "moral" and "conceptual" antitheodicies. See the exchange between Snellman (2019) and Betenson (2019) on this issue; cf. Echazú 2024a.

kind of goods or benefits – such as, again, free will or opportunities for "soul-making" – might outweigh or compensate for the sufferings there are in the world, seeking a divine (or secular) harmony of costs ("prices") and benefits (the good products "purchased"), Phillips objects to "the *concept* of calculation in this context, because it excludes *moral* concepts" (ibid., 158). Theodicism, accordingly, is not simply morally wrong but employs a thoroughly misguided conceptualization of suffering. Even though neither Phillips nor most other Wittgensteinian antitheodicists can be described as transcendental thinkers in anything resembling the Kantian sense of "transcendental," this entanglement of the conceptual and the ethical will be a leading idea in my development of transcendental antitheodicism in Chapter 5.

3.5. Levinasian Antitheodicy

In a quite different tradition, albeit in some ways analogically to Wittgensteinians like Phillips, Emmanuel Levinas – a Lithuanian-born Jewish thinker who was mostly active in France from the 1930s until his death in 1995, having lost his entire family in the Holocaust – formulated a distinctive version of antitheodicy based on his phenomenological articulation of the "uselessness" of suffering and his account of ethics as "first philosophy," culminating in our infinite duty to respond to the face of the other in its vulnerability and mortality.

Because the Holocaust looms large behind all of Levinas's philosophy, and the entire Jewish tradition of antitheodicy that we find centering around his ethical thinking about the other, a caveat is in order. It is of utmost importance to avoid simply using the Holocaust as a practical example in a theoretical study of the problem of evil and suffering (let alone as an instrument serving political goals). Raimond Gaita has a clear-headed warning to make:

> What kind of person would need the Holocaust to raise [the problem of evil and suffering] for him? It would of course almost always be impertinent to question the religious or moral authenticity of those who actually did lose their faith in the camps [...]. But there is something unsavoury in asking in a theoretical way whether the Holocaust should prove that God must lack at least one of the qualities generally attributed to him because the possession of all three[25] looks to be inconsistent with the evil in the world. As though it requires the Holocaust to make the evil in the

---

25 Gaita means, of course, the attributes of omnipotence, omniscience, and absolute goodness, usually employed in a premise in the "argument from evil" (see Chapter 1).

world sufficiently terrible to test the faith of a Jew or a Christian. (Gaita 2000, 149–150.)

There is, then, something potentially morally corrupting (cf. ibid., 150) in the theological use of the Holocaust within a theoretical, intellectualized discussion evaluating theodicy arguments. It is, again, this excessive intellectualization that leads us away from a proper ethical acknowledgment of the suffering other.[26] I believe we should explore the Levinasian antitheodicy against this background: the Holocaust, far from being a mere example in the service of our theoretical pursuits, reminds us how fundamentally important it is to avoid treating the problem of evil and suffering as a theoretical problem to be "solved" (or dissolved) by means of philosophical and theological argumentation. What is at issue is our way of viewing the world, especially the other human being, without any expectation of justificatory theodicies – without, that is, any way of getting rid of the problem. Therefore, self-evidently, if we say (with Levinas) that theodicies are morally impossible after the Holocaust, this does not mean that they would have been possible before the Holocaust.

In what may be considered his key antitheodicist essay, "Useless Suffering," Levinas (2006 [1982], 82) argues that theodicies, seeking to render God innocent, are entirely *disproportional*, out of balance with the sufferings we know from the history of the twentieth century, in particular.[27] He refers approvingly to Kant's reading of the *Book of Job* (see Section 3.1), pointing out, with Kant, that Job "refuses theodicy right to the end" (ibid., 210n9).[28] Far from being justified or rendered meaningful because of some purpose, suffering, according to Levinas, is "for nothing": there is a "depth of meaninglessness" in suffering (ibid., 79). Our duty to attend to the other person's suffering "can be affirmed as the very nexus of human subjectivity," and it is "impossible to question" this "supreme ethical principle" (ibid., 81). It is, moreover, "*my* responsibility for the other, without concern for reciprocity" (ibid., 87), that here points toward the core ideas of Levinas's ethical thinking more generally. Insofar as my obligation to respond to the other's face – the mortal face of a possible victim of suffering – emerges from an appreciation of the meaninglessness ("uselessness") of all suffering, it may be claimed that antitheodicy

---

26 See also the discussion of the entanglement of the theoretical and the practical (also with reference to Primo Levi's Holocaust writings) in Chapter 5.
27 In contrast to this, it might be suggested that the theodicist who employs the Holocaust as an empirical evidential case in a theoretical argument – disregarding the warning by Gaita – treats the Holocaust as "proportional," failing to appreciate the disproportionality which is the heart of the matter.
28 For a useful critical discussion of Levinas's reading of Kant (on Job) on (anti)theodicy, see Davies 2002. On Levinas and antitheodicy, see also, e.g., Sachs 2011.

is central to the Levinasian ethical outlook. This emphasis on antitheodicy makes Levinas one of the most perceptive critics of the tradition of Western philosophy. In "Useless Suffering," we read:

> Perhaps the most revolutionary fact of our twentieth-century consciousness – but it is also an event in Sacred History – is that of the destruction of all balance between Western thought's explicit and implicit theodicy and the forms that suffering and its evil are taking on in the very unfolding of this century. […] [T]he Holocaust of the Jewish people under the reign of Hitler seems to me the paradigm of gratuitous human suffering, in which evil appears in its diabolical horror. […] The disproportion between suffering and every theodicy was shown at Auschwitz with a glaring, obvious clarity. (Ibid., 83–84.)

As noted, Levinas does not mean that theodicies would have been acceptable before the Holocaust and only turned unacceptable "after Auschwitz." On the contrary, the Holocaust stands out as a metonymy of gratuitous human suffering everywhere and always, suffering that cannot possibly be forgiven or reconciled with a generally meaningful world. It is the suffering "for nothing" of the victims that "renders impossible and odious every proposal and every thought that would explain it by the sins of those who have suffered or are dead," and more generally makes the justification of the other's pain an "outrage," "the source of all immorality" (ibid., 84–85). The Holocaust does not merely actually render theodicies false or wrong; more strongly, the "suffering in the other" is "unjustifiable" (not merely unjustified), and the crematoria show theodicy to be "impossible" (ibid., 85). Accordingly, Levinas can be seen as a key figure in the project of developing antitheodicies into what I will (in Chapter 5) call transcendental antitheodicism, pertaining to the necessary conditions for the possibility of having an ethical relation to other human beings in the first place.[29]

It is, then, only in my inescapable ethical relation to the other person that suffering can have any "sense." In a famous passage in his late work, *Otherwise than Being or Beyond Essence*, Levinas writes:

> The vortex – suffering of the other, my pity for his suffering, his pain over my pity, my pain over his pain, etc. – stops at me. The I is what involves one moment more in this iteration. My suffering is the cynosure of all the sufferings – and of all the faults, even of the fault of my persecutors, which amounts to suffering the ultimate persecution, suffering

---

29 For a Kantian transcendental reading of Levinas's concept of the other, see Pöykkö 2023. (I am also indebted to Pöykkö's still unpublished work on Levinas and antitheodicy.)

absolutely. This is not a purifying fire of suffering [...]. The moment of the "for nothing" in suffering is the surplus of non-sense over sense by which the sense of suffering is possible. (Levinas 1987 [1974], 196.)

It is only in the infinite absolute responsibility of the "I" – that is, in my being an ethical subject always having "one degree of responsibility more, the responsibility for the responsibility of the other" (ibid., 117) – that any sense can be attached to suffering. Moreover, this being of the "I" is structured in a primordially antitheodicist manner: we are not who we are (ethical subjects) apart from our always already acknowledging the impossibility of justifying the other's suffering.

Levinas, of course, was only one of the many Jewish philosophers and theologians who spent a considerable part of their life's work seeking to respond ethically to the devastating fact that the Holocaust actually happened.[30] In addition to, for example, the many Jewish mystical theologians who have included antitheodicist ideas in their post-Holocaust reflections (see Garner 2012),[31] a famous Jewish philosopher deserving special mention here is Hans Jonas, who delivered a well-known lecture, "Der Gottesbegriff nach Auschwitz" ("The Concept of God after Auschwitz"), in München in 1984 (see Jonas 1996). In this lecture, he articulates a conception of a processual, finite, and suffering God as the only divinity we may – morally speaking – be able to believe in after the catastrophe of the Holocaust, functioning, of course, metonymically as a shorthand for all unspeakable evil and suffering. Jonas's God is a divinity of "contraction, withdrawal, self-limitation," a God that "renounced his being, divesting himself of his deity," allowing human life and death to emerge in the world (ibid., 134–135, 142). Such a God is

---

30 We should again remember that while antitheodicism, particularly in its Jewish versions, is to a large extent a response to the Holocaust, antitheodicism should reject, as corrupt, the idea that the Holocaust merely serves as a theoretical puzzle in the theodicy discourse. Cf. again Gaita 2000, 149–150; for a discussion of the "unthinkability" of theodicism partly inspired by Gaita, see Pihlström 2025, Chapter 3.
31 See also Pinnock 2002 for a comparative study of Jewish and Christian thinkers seeking responses to the Holocaust that reject theodicies while offering accounts of practical faith and "meaning within suffering." I am not convinced that this project is antitheodicist in my sense, though. The Jewish post-Holocaust ethical tradition, at any rate, is an important attempt to reflect on the compatibility of antitheodicy and religious outlooks on life; no one should claim that these are easy to reconcile, but many Jewish philosophers (including Levinas) have taken crucial steps toward doing so.

"involved" in the suffering of humanity and can be taken to be "run[ning] a risk" in creating the world (ibid., 138).[32]

Significantly for the project of antitheodicy, Jonas emphasizes that the world of suffering – of the kind epitomized in the Holocaust – cannot be harmonized by suggesting that its shocking realities are mere appearances. "[W]e face the terrible truth that the appearance is the reality, and that there is nothing more real than what here appears" – here, that is, in "wasted bodies and distorted faces" and an "utter defilement of humanity" (ibid., 118–119). There is nothing that could be "more real" than the suffering of innocent victims of meaningless evil; this is the reality we must focus on. The Jews murdered in the Holocaust did not die for the sake of their faith, or for the sake of anything. Their absurd deaths were anonymous and inhuman, or dehumanized, and therefore we must rethink our concept of the divinity (if we operate within any theological tradition, such as Judaism), conceived of as "the lord of history" in the Jewish tradition (ibid., 159). From the standpoint of post-Holocaust Jewish antitheodicism, there is little to be said in favor of either traditional theodicies or, say, skeptical theists' speculations about God's possible hidden purposes in allowing suffering.[33]

While the memory of the Holocaust should not be taken to be merely Jewish but, rather, universal (and certainly it should not be politically abused in attacking those who cannot accept Israel's policies), Jewish voices such as Levinas's and Jonas's have offered distinctive perspectives on the development of antitheodicism. A third important Jewish figure I want to mention in this regard is Richard Bernstein. His criticism of theodicies emerges from his learned accounts of thinkers such as Kant, Jonas, Levinas, and Hannah Arendt. Bernstein (2002) joins these philosophers, and the Jewish tradition, in maintaining that any attempt to offer a theodicist justification of evil and suffering, especially of horrendous evils such as the Holocaust but more generally, too, is inevitably morally problematic or even "obscene." Bernstein also carefully analyzes historically developing philosophical accounts of evil, arguing that evil, lacking a permanent core or essence, can always take new

---

32 Interestingly, as I have suggested elsewhere (Pihlström 2014), Jonas's account of the finite God is parallel to James's pragmatist antitheodicism and *its* account of finite divinity, set against the theodicisms of Hegelian absolute idealists (e.g., F.H. Bradley and Josiah Royce) that James, as we saw, criticized (see, e.g., James 1975 [1907], Lectures I and VIII). An important idea shared by James and Jonas, despite their differences, is the irreducibly ethical grounding of this finite metaphysics of the divinity.
33 Critics suggest, however, that Jonas in effect proposes a "new theodicy" in his account of a powerless God (see Agamben 2002 [1999], 20). I will return to the challenge that theodicy may "come back" within antitheodicism in Chapter 5.

forms, spreading everywhere like a fungus (employing Arendt's metaphor), and that therefore our attitude to evil needs continuous rearticulation and critical ethical reflection. It may be suggested that antitheodicism should be a leading idea in this never-ending task of reflection. According to Bernstein, there is a kind of inscrutability in evil due to its lack of essence, and it could be argued that it is important for antitheodicists in particular to acknowledge that gratuitous evil and suffering may always emerge, without any possibility of justification, even amid practices and processes that we might have taken to be protected from them.

We cannot explicitly include Hannah Arendt among "Jewish antitheodicists" here, because it is not easy to find any explicit discussion of theodicies versus antitheodicies in her writing. However, in a broader sense, her conception of the banality of evil, articulated in the famous book, *Eichmann in Jerusalem* (Arendt 1994 [1963]), is, of course, highly relevant to the antitheodicist project – even though there is also a sense in which the banality of evil could even be considered a kind of theodicy because it makes evil intelligible in terms of ordinary human motives (see Neiman 2002, 303; cf. Chignell 2019b, 29–30). More importantly, however, the Kantian criticism of theodicies as failures to acknowledge the fundamental significance of free, autonomous thought – as insincere failures to think – can be compared to the sense in which it is, precisely, the inability to think that characterizes the banality of evil typical of the Eichmanns among us.

We may, finally, highlight the distinctive points in Levinasian antitheodicy by referring to the best-known literary formulation of antitheodicism, Dostoevsky's fictional character Ivan Karamazov. This is because one of the central ideas in the entire Jewish antitheodicist response to the Holocaust is the impossibility of forgiveness, of reconciliation (though we should keep in mind the obvious: Dostoevsky is not a figure in the Jewish tradition, and he wrote several decades before the Holocaust). Dostoevsky's Ivan's revolt against God can be seen as an articulation of Levinas's (2006 [1982], 85) above-cited view that the justification of others' suffering (our "neighbor's pain") is the "source" of all immorality.[34]

As readers of Dostoevsky remember, Ivan Karamazov, in one of the memorable scenes in *The Brothers Karamazov*, "returns his ticket" to God even

---

34 Similar discussions can be found, e.g., in James, who also imagined a case in which the overall well-being and happiness of the universe were "purchased" by condemning one lost soul to eternal torture (see the essay, "The Moral Philosopher and the Moral Life," in James 1979 [1897]). For philosophical discussions of Ivan's criticism of theodicies, see, e.g., Gleeson 2012, and especially Trakakis 2021, to be returned to in Chapter 5. (I am making no historical claims about Levinas's indebtedness to Dostoevsky; I am merely perceiving an analogy here.)

if ultimate redemption and salvation were on offer. This is because we have, according to Ivan, no right to forgive such monstrous actions as those imagined in the novel, for example, deliberately and vengefully causing cruel suffering to a child. Ivan asks whether there is "in all the world" anyone who "could forgive and would have the right to forgive" (Dostoevsky 2003, 320), thus taking extremely seriously the obscenity or scandalousness of theodicies, and what we may (with Levinas) describe as the disproportionality of any such reconciliation and the crime itself. Ivan, in short, is a paradigm of someone who fully understands and appreciates the meaninglessness and "uselessness" of suffering, arguing that no morally decent person sincerely acknowledging others as sharing a "common humanity" (cf. Gaita 2000) and others' distinctive perspectives on the world can possibly forgive the kind of cruelty as a deliberate inflicting of suffering on an innocent child. Whenever we do forgive such atrocities, we are not simply acting immorally but, in a way, stepping beyond the ethical sphere. In particular, when we formulate theodicies in order to make God "innocent" (recall, again, Levinas's formulation), forgiving God the fact that the world is the way it is, or happily exchanging our "ticket" for an admission to an eventual harmony in which everything will be forgiven, we will already have rejected the fundamental ethical task of attending to our fellow human beings. The antitheodicist agrees with Ivan that we cannot possibly forgive God, or history, or anyone or anything, for the reality of the kind of suffering we know to be real. This does not mean that one would have to be an atheist in order to be an antitheodicist; on the contrary, Ivan firmly believes in God's existence (though his view is often called "protest atheism"). He only "returns his ticket," refusing to share any harmonious eternal bliss for which innocent suffering is a price.

In the Jewish tradition, one of the most profound philosophical articulations of the impossibility of forgiveness (again, especially in the context of responding to the Holocaust) was formulated by Vladimir Jankélévitch in his 1967 book, *Le pardon*, in which true or genuine forgiveness is analyzed as taking place only in response to something that is absolutely unforgivable.[35] This is not the place to enter into any further discussion of the concept of forgiveness, which would deserve a study in its own right. Let me simply conclude this chapter by noting that in order to appreciate the basic idea of antitheodicy, especially as it comes up in the Levinasian (or more generally Jewish

---

35 In addition to Jankélévitch's (2005 [1967]) complex work itself, see Udoff 2013 for a rich collection of interpretive essays. Cf. Kivistö and Pihlström 2016, Chapter 3, for a discussion of forgiveness and antitheodicy.

post-Holocaust) tradition, or in Dostoevsky's characters' analogous pained moral and religious struggles, we must take seriously the idea that forgiving (in a standard, ordinary sense) the most horrendous sufferings inflicted on others would itself be an unethical form of theodicy. Questions of forgiveness, then, lead us to the ultimate limits of ethical (and, possibly, religious) thinking. It is part of ethical seriousness to abandon any easy pursuit of ultimate reconciliation, and recognizing this is an essential feature of antitheodicist thinking especially after the Holocaust.

Chapter 4

SECULAR THEODICIES AND CONTEMPORARY ANTITHEODICISM

Moving from a historical sketch of antitheodicies to ongoing contemporary discussions in the philosophy of suffering, we should draw particular attention to the ways in which urgent issues in secular ethics can be interpreted in terms of (anti)theodicy. An introduction to secular theodicism and antitheodicism is therefore needed. Here my discussion primarily takes its departure from a broadly pragmatist understanding of ethics and the (anti)theodicy debate (see Section 3.3 for pragmatist antitheodicy), but all the historical versions of antitheodicy flowing from Kant, discussed in the previous chapter, should be considered relevant to the contemporary developments – especially because contemporary antitheodicisms should be understood as neutral with respect to any religious or theological commitments, and because it was Kant who turned our attention from metaphysical theodicies concerned with excusing God to an essentially ethical approach to evil and suffering in terms of practical reason. In particular, appreciating the broader relevance of antitheodicism in contemporary philosophy presupposes that we reach far beyond the philosophy of religion as the traditional core area of the theodicy discussion (without, of course, neglecting to develop antitheodicies in that special field, too).

4.1. Secular Theodicism and Antitheodicism: A Pragmatist Line of Inquiry

Considering secular theodicies and theodicism may remind us that if we lack a sufficient awareness of the theodicist tendencies of our practices of moral and political reasoning and of the social norms and institutions based on such practices, we, as individuals and societies, fall dramatically short of appropriately appreciating the kind of depth that serious ethical questions about human life, suffering, and death involve. Here, of course, we can only approach these enormous themes in very broad strokes. In any case, in this sense, our problem with theodicies and theodicism is "metaethical" – raising fundamental questions about the "meaning" of the ethical stance to the world in general and to other human beings in particular. This does not mean that, say, pragmatist criticism of secular theodicies would be "metaethical" in the sense in which this word is used in contemporary analytic metaethics, though. Rather, we need to start from the hypothesis that identifying and analyzing the mostly implicit secular theodicism of our practices and reasoning patterns (often manifested in public discussions) is a way of making explicit the true practical significance of antitheodicism in social ethics and politics in our times. As both mainstream normative ethics and metaethics today arguably fail in appropriately responding to this need of understanding secular theodicism, the conceptual innovations needed here would be of the magnitude of, say, Arendt's concept of the banality of evil, James's and other pragmatists' meliorism (briefly discussed in Chapter 3), or even Kant's seminal idea of the "radicality" of evil as an inclination "rooted" in humanity. Therefore, an examination of contemporary secular (anti)theodicism such as the one in this chapter is only the beginning of what ought to turn into a comprehensive inquiry into our engagement with suffering.

More concretely, the general aims of the kind of investigation I think we need would be to sharpen the definition of secular theodicy and theodicism; to identify some of the most important types of secular theodicy; to develop a systematic and widely applicable (secular) antitheodicist approach, primarily based on pragmatism but utilizing conceptual and argumentative resources from Kantian, Wittgensteinian, and other relevant orientations in modern philosophy (including pragmatist and transcendental methodologies, as outlined in Chapter 2); and to use this approach to critically analyze the ethical assumptions of theodicies, especially in their secular forms, and to find ways of avoiding the theodicist tendencies of our practices as far as possible. The main hypothesis from which such inquiry could begin is that antitheodicism is necessary for ethical decency within the discourses on suffering we constantly need to engage in in our troubled world and in practices informed by those discourses (see further Chapter 5). More specific research questions and hypotheses could include, among others, the following.

First, there are *conceptual, theoretical, and metaphysical questions* to be asked. Are secular theodicies dependent on, for example, (some version of) the principle of sufficient reason or other metaphysical background assumptions?[1] Related questions could focus on the critique of optimism (cf., again, van

---

1 For such metaphysical and meta-metaphysical inquiries into the background assumptions of theodicies, see Snellman 2023.

der Lugt 2021, 2025, and Chapters 2–3): Why and how exactly is optimism an ethically pernicious philosophy, also to be avoided in political contexts? The explicit or implicit theodicism of optimist worldviews and political ideologies may be analyzed at individual and cultural levels and subjected to pragmatist meliorist antitheodicist critique. Furthermore, we may ask whether pragmatist articulations of antitheodicism, such as those presented by James (see Chapter 3), can be reinterpreted as Kantian-like transcendental arguments. How, in particular, are they related to transcendental elements in other antitheodicist approaches in contemporary philosophy, such as Wittgensteinian and Levinasian ones? The human-scale perspective on suffering inherent in antitheodicism may finally lead us to investigate whether theodicism is necessarily committed to (theological or secular versions of) an in- or superhuman "God's-Eye View," to be critically countered by a humanistic emphasis on inescapable human finitude (cf. Pihlström 2020a, Chapter 4, and 2023, Chapter 5). It may be argued that suffering is a human problem, not God's moral problem. How, then, is this humanism related to, say, metaphysical questions of realism and naturalism? How does it figure in antitheodicist critique of, for example, utilitarian ethics allegedly calculatingly "measuring" sufferings?

Secondly, there are *"applied" ethical, cultural, and societal questions* that also need to be asked. What kind of secular theodicies and antitheodicies might be identified in modern fictional literature, film, and the other arts? How, for instance, does literature deal with teleological views on the alleged meaning or purpose of suffering when addressing ethical and political issues of contemporary societies? More concretely, what kind of secular theodicies and antitheodicies can be identified in media and social media debates over the past several years on, say, the Covid-19 pandemic, the Russian invasion of Ukraine in 2022, the Israeli campaign in Gaza taking genocidal dimensions since the attack by Hamas in 2023, and the global crisis emerging from these and other wars? Furthermore, do philosophical, historical, and political interpretations of, say, war and genocide involve theodicist assumptions? How exactly can and should they be subjected to antitheodicist critique? In particular, is the classical just war theory essentially (secularly) theodicist?[2]

By investigating questions such as these (which, of course, we cannot do here at any length), a thoroughgoing pragmatist interpretation and critique of secular theodicism could provide a dramatically enhanced understanding of the prevalence of the phenomenon of secular theodicy relevant not only to academic theorization but also to public discussions. Such investigations

---

2 This issue will be considered as a brief case study toward the end of this chapter.

could even lead to novel philosophical conceptualizations of the ethical standards of discourses on suffering and the nature of ethics and ethical problems generally, because applying the conceptual machinery of antitheodicism to secular responses to suffering could amount to a major rearticulation of what we take to be the existential significance (or, indeed, meaninglessness) of suffering and of our ethical obligation to respond to it. Therefore, serious reflection on these themes might even transform our received philosophical understanding of the entire issue of suffering, significantly renewing the conceptual and argumentative frameworks and resources we employ in analyzing, and responding to, pain and evil. This is why secular antitheodicy *matters*.

It is, moreover, methodologically vitally important to develop a pragmatist antitheodicism based on (broadly) transcendental argumentation – as will be further discussed in the next chapter. In particular, such an inquiry might focus on the relation between antitheodicism and the concept of the ethically "unthinkable" as framing the area of *possible* ethical debate and inquiry, arguing for a cultural shift from the idea that rejecting theodicies would be culturally unthinkable (a widely assumed early modern view) to the position that subscribing to theodicism, even secularly, is itself ethically unthinkable.[3] At the meta-level, the criteria and limits of sound argument inevitably become an issue here. Philosophers examining the distinction between what is considered ("merely") ethically wrong and what is ruled out as unthinkable, where such ruling out constitutes the area within which distinguishing between right and wrong is possible in the first place (cf. Pihlström 2025), are at least implicitly exploring the limits of our ethical decency, and the critique of secular theodicism may be a key element of such an exploration.

As antitheodicism may (I am suggesting) significantly transform the ways we think about evil, suffering, and ethical responsibility, its potential impact on our individual and social lives is enormous. This is, however, a long-term matter, as is any "impact" that philosophical reflections might have. Despite the wide relevance of secular theodicies and their critique, no immediate applications of philosophical ideas to practical social life should be expected. Yet, developing antitheodicism as a general ethical approach could be highly relevant to assessing the ways we as individuals and societies discuss the meaningfulness and meaninglessness of suffering – in secular or religious terms. In particular, one may demonstrate the ethically problematic nature of theodicism by applying the theodicy versus antitheodicy debate to real-life cases,

---

3 I am borrowing the concept of the "unthinkable" from Gaita 2004 [1991], Chapter 17. Gaita does not explicitly discuss theodicies as unthinkable, though. See further Chapter 5.

suggesting ways out of the predicament defined by theodicism. Such inquiries could be extended to show that theodicism is implicit in controversies on health-care ethics (including but not restricted to Covid-19-related contexts), on individual and social welfare, on whether historical sufferings serve meaningful purposes, and on the just distribution of the costs of the transitions needed for responding to the climate crisis – to name only a few obvious areas of application (keeping in mind, again, that the issue of overarching justification of suffering in its theodicist sense does not trivially reduce to the phenomenon of "double effects"). At the same time, we should do our best to develop our self-critical capabilities of recognizing how difficult it is to abandon theodicist assumptions. Accordingly, secular antitheodicist critique may have a tremendous effect on how taking the theodicy issue seriously will change our conceptualization not only of academic problems in the philosophy of religion but also our ethical stance to public debates on, for example, Covid-19 or other pandemics, the climate crisis, and the devastating wars of our times. Far from being a marginal problem in theology and the philosophy of religion, the problem of evil and suffering and the conflict between theodicism and antitheodicism may thus be argued to lie at the center of our attempts to lead decent lives, individually and socially. Constructing such an argument aims at enabling us to recognize this fact about the *inescapability* of the theodicy issue in our culture – and the pragmatically vital need for a transcendental antitheodicist assessment, a critique penetrating into our most fundamental assumptions concerning what is constitutive of our ethical standpoint.

Pragmatist antitheodicism, transcendentally developed (and thus inspired by Kantian antitheodicy), not only takes seriously the need to critically consider theodicies and theodicism as morally problematic but also avoids dealing with them in a moralizing way. The question is not about the choice between "moral" and "conceptual" antitheodicies[4] but about the sense in which theodicism ("conceptually") leads us beyond the sphere of serious moral discussion. From the standpoint of pragmatist-cum-transcendental antitheodicism, theodicies are not just wrong (let alone "false" in any straightforward sense) but in some sense ethically impossible or unthinkable – or, in other words, distortions of our ethical decency or seriousness (as will be further argued in Chapter 5). They deprive us of the possibility of sincere ethical conceptualization of suffering, making it impossible for us to truly engage in the practices of ethically attending to the experiences of the victims of suffering. In order for

---

4 See again Snellman 2023, as well as Snellman's (2019) exchange with Betenson (2019) on this issue.

us to be able to participate in honest ethical and political discussion based on the acknowledgment that people suffer enormously and meaninglessly, theodicies (both religious and secular) must, arguably, be ruled out in advance rather than theoretically considered or even taken seriously. Here this pragmatic-transcendental argument remains very sketchy, but it is in this spirit that the critique of secular theodicies and theodicism in my view needs to be developed (and will be developed in this chapter and the next one), albeit with full awareness of the impossibility of ever completely eradicating the theodicist assumptions deeply rooted in our thinking. This, however, is only to formulate a highly tentative project of antitheodicist critical inquiry. Most of the questions listed above would require much more than a short book to be even properly raised, let alone comprehensively examined. Let me therefore move on from a general draft of a line of inquiry to concrete case studies of secular theodicism relevant to an ethical understanding of our contemporary world.

4.2. Secular (Anti)theodicy at Work

Consider again a familiar case: the Covid-19 pandemic. Thinking about the ethical dimensions of the political decisions made in response to the spread of the dangerous virus, I suppose it is obvious, for most of us, that it was, and would always be, wrong to simply "sacrifice" (for an allegedly greater cause) the elderly and other risk groups who may die due to catching the virus. However, by putting societies into a lockdown (as we clearly had to do especially before the vaccines were developed in 2020), we also caused enormous economic and social trouble to many people for a long time. Such hardships may in the long run also lead to other illnesses and even deaths, or at least to major sufferings, and thus we, or political decision-makers in particular, unavoidably have to weigh the disadvantages of the lockdown against the threat of the virus. Cases like this – even if they are dealt with through entirely democratic processes – result in difficult political tensions and disagreements, as we know.[5] While it is, of course, not at all straightforward to suggest any specifically antitheodicist way of dealing with such issues, the theodicist tendencies in our thinking about such matters need to be fully recognized.

Instead of providing any simple solutions, the antitheodicist perspective emphasizes our continuous duty to be self-critically aware of our inescapable temptation to view some sufferings as "legitimate prices" to be "paid" for avoiding some other kinds of sufferings. This way of thinking is *per se*

---

5 For discussions of Covid-19 and democracy explicitly from the perspective of secular theodicy, see Bosman and van Wieringen 2021; Montanye 2024.

problematic,[6] even if unavoidable, and succumbing to theodicist arguments such as the Leibnizian best possible world theodicy – however logically impeccable they might seem to be – contributes to the legitimation of such theodicy-driven ways of thinking in delicate ethical contexts in which they should not be seen as unproblematic at all. The most important message of the antitheodicist approach in cases like this is that it is never innocent to find some moral course of action acceptable simply because it is the "lesser evil" compared to its alternatives. We may, as we surely did in the pandemic (not to mention horrors like the Holocaust), arrive at situations in which no decent solution is available.

The theodicist logic of Covid-19 measures – both imposing restrictions and lifting them – reminds us that we are, when discussing suffering and its justification, primarily dealing with problems of the human world. Again, this leads us to emphasize the secular dimensions of the theodicy issue. It is crucial to observe that antitheodicist ethical critique – *even* in the context of religious and/or theological formulations of the problem of suffering – is *not* directed at God and does not even have to take any stand whatsoever regarding the question concerning God's existence, even though that is the traditional question defining theodicist arguments and counterarguments. Antitheodicism is a genuine option for a modern thinker for whom it is no longer similarly a genuine option to find God's existence self-evident in the way Job still does in his revolt against God (and even Ivan Karamazov does). Job (initially) takes God to be a person one may meaningfully morally revolt against, and similarly theistic theodicists today assume that we can evaluate God's moral standing, for example, in terms of the Leibnizian "best possible world" theodicy (see, e.g., Franklin 2020). For antitheodicists, this is hard to take seriously, and we may say that Job himself learns – upon hearing God's speech – that God is *not* a morally responsible person in the way human beings must be taken to be.[7] In brief, it makes little sense to claim God, as absolutely sovereign, to be morally responsible to anyone or anything.

---

6 As noted in Chapter 2, the vocabulary of "price" suggests that sufferings can be "measured" and rendered commensurate with each other, whereas antitheodicism can be taken to deny this (cf. Saarinen 2019).
7 This could also be regarded as the thrust of the Kantian antitheodicist critique culminating in Kant's reading of the *Book of Job* (see Chapter 3): the human virtues of sincerity and honesty, and the corresponding vices of insincerity and dishonesty, rather than metaphysical commitments to God's existence or non-existence, are at the core of our assessment of how to respond to suffering. For some criticism of Franklin's defense of theodicies, see Chapter 5.

Whether or not God exists, we human beings are responsible not only for what we do when encountering others' suffering but also for the discourses through which we respond to evil and suffering around us, even if those discourses do involve the concept of God. Our belief or disbelief in God's reality may shape and color our responses, but the opposition between theodicism and antitheodicism as such remains neutral with regard to the question of theism and atheism (cf. again Chapter 2). This I take to be a fundamental observation about our contemporary secular (anti)theodicy discourse. Moreover, as we have seen, just as there can be secular theodicies, there may be theistic or religious forms of antitheodicism (along with secular ones, of course), even though, admittedly, classical forms of theism may be difficult to integrate with resolute antitheodicism due to the deep historical entanglement of particularly Christian theology with theodicy.[8] At least in principle, a religious believer may very well resort to their own understanding of the divinity, and perhaps critically rethink that understanding (e.g., along the lines suggested in Jonas's rethinking of God "after Auschwitz," briefly discussed in Chapter 3), in an attempt to develop a thoroughly antitheodicist account of evil and suffering with no divine or secular justification for suffering. This is because antitheodicism, as repeatedly explained, does not simply amount to the rejection of theodicies – any particular theodicies or theodicies in general – but, rather, to an attempt to turn the entire discussion away from the pursuit of theodicies. This turn itself can utilize any conceptual resources that are philosophically (or theologically) available, including the concept of God and other concepts derivable from religious and theological traditions, though we must acknowledge that it may not be an easy task.

While there is typically a teleological structure in religious theodicies (see, e.g., Trakakis 2018, 365), the concept of a secular theodicy cannot be simply reduced to the idea that suffering is legitimized in social practices with reference to some particular aim or goal. Such legitimization can take different shapes in different political or other contexts. A more comprehensive discussion of these matters would have to explore, say, the similarities and differences between quasi-theodicist teleology-driven ethical and political arguments we might be tempted to adopt in various contexts, ranging from

---

8 As we saw in Chapter 3, many of the leading antitheodicists in the history of modern philosophy – Kant, James, Levinas, and Wittgensteinians like D.Z. Phillips – maintained at least neutral or sympathetic, and in any case not hostile, attitudes toward religious beliefs and traditions. Antitheodicism in this sense does not emerge from the atheist criticism of theodicies but on the contrary from an attempt to find an ethically decent religious way of living with suffering. (For theistic antitheodicies, see, e.g., Roth 2004.)

Covid-19 restrictions and prioritization issues in health care generally to, say, political or economic responses to the climate crisis, a variety of political decisions both causing and trying to prevent forms of "social suffering," as well as, at a certain extreme, considerations of "excusable casualties" in attempts to wage a just war. Let me, before moving on to a slightly more detailed case study of secular theodicy and antitheodicy, mention a few examples all of which would deserve lengthy comments and discussion.

First, for an illustrative political case, consider Tony Judt's (1992) profound analysis of how post-WWII French intellectuals (including, most famously, Jean-Paul Sartre but many others as well) were unable to drop their faith in the historical meaningfulness of communism despite the enormous suffering that Soviet communists, in particular, inflicted on obviously innocent victims. The potential for further philosophical analysis of such cases of what Judt calls "intellectual irresponsibility" in terms of the distinction between theodicism and antitheodicism is enormous. The world-historical teleology of communism was, for most French intellectuals, the ultimate justification for the undeniably unjust experiences the victims had to go through. Sartre, Maurice Merleau-Ponty, and many others were, according to Judt, committed to an essentially historical argument whose core was the need to view our lives and our history as meaningful; it was considered unimaginable that history would have no purpose (ibid., 120–121). Just as the resolute religious (theistic, e.g., Christian) theodicist will not give up their faith in divine providence come what may, Sartre never abandoned his faith in the historical truth of communism (ibid., 123).[9] Judt reminds us about one important exception, though: Albert Camus. One factor in his conflict with Sartre was Camus's finding it necessary to emphasize our responsibility to other human beings in contrast to our responsibility to the alleged teleological structure of history, or the pre-established truth of any ideology, even communism (see ibid., 121).[10] Unlike Sartre, Camus can, arguably, be rather naturally interpreted as an antitheodicist writer.[11] Camus can certainly be placed among those modern thinkers – "existentialists" in a broad sense (cf. Trakakis 2023) – who challenged not only theistic theodicies but any "idealist" (e.g., Hegelian) promises

---

9 See further Judt 1992, 137–138, on the romanticization of the suffering of the victims of communism among the French intellectuals.
10 Judt (1992, 184–185) also points out that Sartre's famous criticism of antisemitism contains no discussion of communist antisemitism.
11 For an excellent analysis of Camus as a political antitheodicist, see Rakhmanin 2024. The key work discussed by Rakhmanin in this regard is, of course, *The Plague* (see also Pihlström and Kivistö 2023, Chapter 3), but an antitheodicist tendency can be seen to extend through Camus's defense of humanity throughout his work.

of a harmonious metaphysical system that would theodicistically accommodate all suffering.¹²

Secondly, a very different example of secular theodicy emerges from Austrian Holocaust survivor Viktor Frankl's notion of the "will to meaning." According to Frankl, some concentration camp prisoners' ability to continue to view their lives as meaningful contributed positively to their chances of surviving, and this idea later formed the basis of Frankl's famous logotherapy. In contrast, another – clearly more antitheodicistically inclined – Holocaust survivor, Primo Levi, described the camps in terms of a devastating destruction of meanings, or even the destruction of our very capacities of meaningfulness or meaning-making.¹³ If we regard Frankl's (e.g., 1969) concept of the "will to meaning" as analogous to what William James (1979 [1897]) called the "will to believe," the question arises whether even James – who can be generally considered an antitheodicist, as we saw in Chapter 3 – presupposed at least traces of theodicism in his conception of our right to embrace a religious hypothesis if faced with a "genuine option" upon which our ability to experience our lives as meaningful, or worth living, depends.¹⁴ Within American pragmatism, not only Dewey, whose progressivism and apparent lack of sufficient attention to the tragic aspects of human lives and history could be argued to make him, at least potentially, a secular theodicist, but even James, the resolute pragmatist antitheodicist, would then have to be interpreted as remaining partly committed to theodicist ideas.¹⁵

Furthermore, thirdly, Luca Mavelli (2016) interestingly proposes to find a secular theodicy (using these explicit terms) at work in what he calls the governance of uncertainty "in a secular age": a kind of rationalization of the processes of "securitization" and criminalization of entire groups of people takes place, we are told, through a Foucauldian "biopolitical logic" replacing traditional theodicies with a secular "theodicy of good fortune" (or "sociodicy")

---

12 Distinguishing between "idealism" and "existentialism" in this sense, Trakakis (2023) includes thinkers such as Dostoevsky, Kierkegaard, Nietzsche, and Kafka, along with Camus, in the latter tradition. On Hegel (as well as Marx) as committed to theodicy, see also Neiman 2019, 371–372.

13 In addition to Levi's canonical writings (e.g., Levi 1976 [1958]), see Phillips 2005 for a critique of Frankl's account of the possibility of voluntary meaning-making even in the camps.

14 However, the Jamesian "will to believe" idea itself can also be employed to defend antitheodicism, as suggested in Pihlström 2021, Chapter 6.

15 See Noddings 2018, especially 29–30, 39, for a discussion of Dewey relevant to these concerns: Dewey "had no patience with theodicy" and identified evil with pain and injustice in the world, but he has also been criticized for remaining too optimistic in his faith in science, progress, and education.

quasi-justifying the divisions between the fortunate and the suffering, also highly problematically flirting with the traditional theodicist project of rendering all suffering meaningful, albeit in the absence of any transcendence. Mavelli goes rather far, however, in viewing this modern secularized theodicy as culminating in torture, because the very same modern processes of governance that he claims to yield quasi-theodicist torture also deal with torture as, for example, a war crime. Even so, it is important to draw attention to the ways in which theodicist logic may implicitly define relatively normal (even if not perfectly everyday) social, political, and administrative discourses.[16]

All these cases of secular theodicies (merely listed here as examples), and many others, need ethically grounded antitheodicist critique. They may also motivate pursuing the kind of questions (both metaphysical and ethical, or "applied") formulated in Section 4.1. After having had a glimpse of the remarkable variety of secular theodicies and having (I hope) perceived the need for antitheodicist critique employing the resources of the historical traditions of antitheodicy introduced in the previous chapter, I next propose to consider in some more detail one specific example of considerable contemporary relevance, namely, the ethics of war and peace. I am not suggesting that the traditional problems of, say, the just war theory (or, mutatis mutandis, pacifism) could be easily resolved by adopting the conceptual framework of secular theodicy versus antitheodicy, but I hope this case study can further encourage us to articulate that framework.

4.3. A Case Study: On the Theodicism of the Just War Theory

In our violent and dangerous world, it may be argued that pacifist appeals to peace are either trivial (everyone in their right mind wishes we could live in peace) or misguided (because we cannot accept any obviously unjust peace – as in the case of the current Ukrainian war, in which peace at the moment of this writing in 2025, after more than three years of devastating unprovoked war criminally launched by Russia in 2022, could pragmatically amount to Russia's victory). The critic of (radical) pacifism may find it astonishing how otherwise reasonable people have, for example, argued against Finland and Sweden joining NATO without duly acknowledging that their own freedom to speak for peace is protected by NATO and thus ultimately by nuclear

---

16 Or at least the margins or limits of such normality: see Derrida's (2004) proposal to view capital punishment as a "temptation of theodicy." On sociological reinterpretations of theodicy, see Morgan and Wilkinson 2001.

deterrence.[17] It seems more obvious than ever, even for us Europeans, that only by maintaining sufficiently strong military capabilities can we hope to secure peace in the world we live in. Now, though all of this may be taken to be rather self-evident, the just war theory, implicitly invoked in the idea that it would be permissible (and even a duty) for the NATO allies to defend themselves and one another (and thus their democratic institutions, human rights, and the rule of law) in case of military aggression, is not only an influential but also a complex and problematic tradition in Western philosophy and may be critically scrutinized in terms of the secular theodicy discussion. The ethical and intellectual project of justifying war may in the end be as uncritical as naïve pacifism is, and the reason for this is its implicit reliance on a form of secular theodicism – or so I will suggest in this section.

I believe we need to problematize the idea that war could *simply* be morally justified, though in some cases a "just war" may be an excusable way of pursuing fundamental ethical and political goals, such as the goal of maintaining a decent democratic society. Ukraine has over the past years continued to fight (with Western support) not only to defend its existence as a sovereign nation but also for the continuation of the liberal democratic way of life and the institutions of democratic governance, human rights, and the rule of law against an existential threat caused by a murderous terror regime. It would be obviously wrong to fight this war by launching nuclear missiles toward Moscow, but it is (I think a decent person should say) in some sense clearly permissible for Ukraine and its allies to engage in defensive actions, at least within the Ukrainian territory, against the Russian invasion. Importantly, this is something that can be done only by doing (even great) evil, that is, by killing as many invading combatants as possible and thus causing them and their families enormous suffering.

It would not only be morally (and, of course, politically) wrong to claim that Ukraine does not have the right to self-defense, or to claim Ukraine to be unwilling to achieve peace due to its willingness to continue fighting in the interest of securing a peace that would at least be an acceptable compromise and not completely unjust. It could be suggested that it is, much more importantly, indecent or even unthinkable to claim that we ("the West") should simply "sacrifice" Ukraine's right to remain a nation for the "mere" goal of maintaining peace at all costs. Such an immoral sacrifice would arguably

---

17 At the time of this writing (2025), the future of NATO is, of course, somewhat uncertain, as the relations between the United States and its European allies are undergoing transformation. The basic idea of NATO and its member states' commitment to it remains unchanged, though.

undermine the value of the peace to be achieved, which would in such a scenario hardly be a genuine peace in any case but just an opportunity for the enemy to continue the war later. It is not morally decent to be a (radical) pacifist, if this argument is correct, at least insofar as pacifism maintains that it is never acceptable to wage war, even defensive war.[18] Sacrificing Ukraine – finding Ukraine's existence as a nation a price to be paid for the greater good of ending war – would not only destroy the Ukrainian nation but *us* as a moral community. I would strongly hesitate to straightforwardly call pacifism evil, though. It might be better to call it (like theodicism) illusory or even ethically unthinkable (cf. Pihlström 2025, Chapter 5), at least in certain contexts. Absolute pacifism is something that cannot be seriously considered in a situation that, for example, the decent peoples of the world found themselves in when they had to resist the Nazis' genocidal war of destruction more than 80 years ago.

How exactly should we assess the just war theory in the context of our investigation of secular theodicies?[19] It would be impossible here to dwell on the complex history of theories of just war. For our modern world, this history unfolds from Augustine through Thomas Aquinas and early modern thinkers like Francisco Suarez and Hugo Grotius up to theories on the brink of modernity such as, perhaps most importantly, Kant's view on "perpetual peace." It was Michael Walzer (1992 [1977]) who largely revived this discussion in contemporary ethics and political philosophy. His views on what constitutes just war are by no means universally accepted,[20] but in order to connect this

---

18 This is compatible with acknowledging that pacifism as a wider critical ethical and social theory also has its benefits, even though as an absolute refusal to accept violence in any situation it cannot be seriously considered. See, e.g., Fiala 2018. This is not the place to explore the complexities of pacifism.
19 For significant contemporary contributions to the just war theory, see, e.g., Walzer 1992 [1977] and McMahan 2009.
20 For example, McMahan (2009, 112–115) vigorously challenges Walzer's views on "the moral equality of combatants." Generally, McMahan is highly critical of standard assumptions of the just war theory, arguing that it is always wrong to fight in an unjust war and that even in war killing is immoral unless self-defensive (and that when one is fighting an unjust war, killing is wrong even when self-defensive, because by engaging in an unjust war, the combatants have made themselves liable to be killed and have given up their moral right to self-defense). For our discussion here, it is not necessary to determine exactly how the distinction between just and unjust wars is drawn; the key issue for us is that regardless of how it is drawn, even the most obviously just wars might be only quasi-theodicistically justified (which, however, is not to claim that we should never engage in war but that whenever we must do so, we must be aware of the inescapability of a theodicist logic of justification). Fiala (2010 xi–xii, 180–181) also

topic with our main issue in this investigation, I am here briefly referring to Walzer simply because of the wide impact of his work.

It might be argued that the idea of just war is inherently (secularly) theodicist: the evil done even by the right-minded fighting for a just cause can only be legitimized, or excused, in terms of a theodicy-like teleological narrative referring to the ultimate benefits of waging war. The good cause, such as saving Ukraine as a sovereign nation and respecting the human rights of its citizens, justifies the killing of the invaders. Interestingly, however, Raimond Gaita (2004 [1991], Chapter 14) maintains that pacifism and the critique of pacifism are not in the end a matter of justification, because the fact that we *will* do evil if necessary – if the conditions of our ethical and political communality are threatened – is constitutive of "us," and therefore the pacifist (rather than being naïve or simply a free-rider) is not "fully amongst us," failing to join "us" in recognizing the constitutive nature of the fact that we will do evil if those conditions are indeed under serious threat.[21] In this sense, Gaita's criticism of pacifism is not an instance of the just war theory and thus not necessarily based on theodicism of any kind. In contrast to his relatively complex position taking a critical stance to the very project of justification, the more traditional theorization on just war – as humanly important as it is – runs the risk of ending up with theodicism, or some form of secular theodicy. Let us hear what Walzer has to say:

> What does it mean *not to have died in vain?* There must be purposes that are worth dying for, outcomes for which soldiers' lives are not too high a price. The idea of a just war requires the same assumption. A just war is one that it is morally urgent to win, and a soldier who dies in a just war does not die in vain. (Walzer 1992 [1977], 110, original emphasis.)

A just war against an aggressor that threatens, for example, the deepest values of political independence and international order – an aggressor such as Nazi Germany with which peace negotiations would have been unthinkable – may even require fighting until the final end of unconditional surrender (see ibid., 113), despite enormous casualties. According to a theodicist construal of just war, the immeasurably important goal of this fighting justifies or at least excuses the lost lives and other sufferings that need to be "paid" as a "price" for the outcome, and possibly even actions that would otherwise be

---

interestingly maintains that the just war theory only works together with some form of theodicy.
21 For a critical discussion of Gaita's quasi-transcendental anti-pacifist argumentation, see Pihlström 2025, Chapter 5.

considered evil. The sufferings that combatants engaging in a just war go through are therefore "meaningful" or "purposive," playing a role in an overall scheme of political and historical if not cosmic or religious significance.[22]

This takes us to one of Walzer's best-known concepts, "supreme emergency." Paradigmatically, "Nazism was an ultimate threat to everything decent in our lives," "evil objectified in the world," and therefore fighting against it was the only conceivable choice (ibid., 253).[23] The unthinkability of not fighting against Nazism was based on it being "literally unbearable" that the Nazis would have won and enslaved or massacred the entire humankind (see ibid., 254).[24] Hence supreme emergency, and hence even the (in other contexts unthinkable) decision to bomb German civilians and thus to intentionally violate the rules of war (ibid., 259). In Gaita's terms, the relations between morality, politics, and law can be highly complex, and all of these belong within "the ethical"; thus, sometimes morality has to yield when other ethical considerations overrule it (see again Gaita 2004 [1991], Chapter 10). As Walzer (1992 [1977], 260) points out, there are cases of supreme emergency where we (or I, as a person) must "accept the burdens of criminality here and now." We might have to accept illegality or immorality in order to win a just war that is truly urgent to win due to its causing us a supreme emergency. However, this by no means justifies or even excuses, say, all or even any of the terror bombings by the Allies toward the end of World War

---

22 This is compatible with maintaining that, in many cases, we cannot easily decide whether a given war is just. What matters, theoretically, is just that there are actual or at least possible cases in which waging war may be justified in terms of its expected outcome.

23 Walzer (1992 [1977], 253) here specifically says that "there could never have been anything to do but fight against it." I read this as suggesting that fighting against Nazism was not even a genuine choice. The pacifists among us – just as those of "us" who did fight against Nazism – only had an illusion of choice. They did not really suggest an alternative course of action for anyone involved, at least not for those who could be taken to be, or remain, genuinely among us. Anyone who maintained that it was not necessary, or not worth the trouble, to fight against the Nazis disqualified as "one of us." (I would be tempted to say that something analogous holds today about our relation to Putin's Russia. We have no real choice but to do everything within our power to oppose its aggressive imperialism and war crimes.)

24 Walzer (1992 [1977], 254) writes: "For the survival and freedom of political communities – whose members share a way of life, developed by their ancestors, to be passed on to their children – are the highest values of international society." Thus, sharing a "way of life" is something that simply must be defended (or, better, *is* defended by the sharers.

II when everything was, militarily speaking, clear.[25] In any case, fighting for what we must fight for (or simply do, having no choice) may require us to make considerable moral sacrifices. Politicians, in particular, usually have no alternative but to think in a utilitarian way – which, on the other hand, does not mean that they would be "free of guilt" when doing so (see ibid., 326). Utilitarianism may be ethically wrong or even unthinkable due to its tendency to sacrifice innocents, if necessary, but it may at the same time be politically – and thus in a broad sense ethically – unavoidable. This is one example of the way in which theodicism enters a fully secular ethical and political discussion.

The situation can be conceptualized in terms of secular theodicism reaching out toward a "higher" perspective of ultimate meaningfulness, which legitimizes sacrificing innocents in the interest of protecting something fundamentally important. Alternatively, however, it can be approached in terms of an antitheodicist acknowledgment of our never being free from guilt, no matter what we do. Insofar as theodicism itself is taken to be ethically indecent, a violation of the necessary conditions for the possibility of the ethical stance, we should do everything we can to develop the theory of just war into an antitheodicist rather than theodicist direction. But the tension certainly remains within the entire paradigm. It may be challenging not to construe the concept of a just war in a (secularly) quasi-theodicist manner, but this is not to say it is impossible. In order to reflect on when and how, if ever, war can or might be justified, or at least excusable, we must try to avoid theodicist accounts of the just war whenever we can.

The contingency and historical relativity of the boundary between the ethically thinkable and the unthinkable (cf. Pihlström 2025) is a fundamental issue here, and it is at this (in my view transcendental) level that the key

---

25 The concept of supreme emergency also plays a role in Walzer's analysis of the complex issue of nuclear deterrence (urgently relevant again as Russia threatens the civilized world with nuclear weapons): "Supreme emergency has become a permanent condition. Deterrence is a way of coping with that condition, and though it is a bad way, there may well be no other that is practical in a world of sovereign and suspicious states. We threaten evil in order not to do it, and the doing of it would be so terrible that the threat seems in comparison to be morally defensible" (Walzer 1992 [1977], 274). Walzer further maintains that nuclear weapons change the ethics of war so completely that they "explode the theory of just war" (ibid., 282). There is no way in which nuclear war (any more than, say, genocide) could ever be morally acceptable or even excusable – but admitting this is only the beginning of the ethical debate on deterrence (which I am unable to engage in here). Those who *simply* maintain that nuclear deterrence is always wrong do not seem to fully appreciate what kind of world we are living in.

ethical import of the just war theory and ethical debates on pacifism also ought to be examined. Even if the entire humankind contingently agreed about some moral principle – even if they all turned Nazis – we can say (now that we are here to say it) that this would be impossible or unthinkable ("for us"). If *we* became Nazis, we would do (or would have done) the unthinkable, even though this would of course *then* no longer be unthinkable for us anymore. What is ethically thinkable and unthinkable (for us) cannot be contingently decided by voting, for example, nor by any matter-of-factual moral agreement, no matter how widespread or even universal. Yet even a transcendental examination of the boundaries of the thinkable that are presupposed in our engaging in serious moral discussion at all has to take place with full acknowledgment of the ultimate contingency of the most deeply embedded constitutive necessities of our form of life, including what might be described (anticipating the discussion of Chapter 5) the transcendental ethical necessity of avoiding theodicist justifications of suffering. Our drawing the (or some) boundary between the thinkable and the unthinkable, though itself contingent upon our actually drawing it, plays a transcendental role in enabling serious moral discussion, even if in the end it is merely a local (namely, our) way of doing something that we contingently can do or fail to do. This relatively abstract point holds about our historically contextualized, and shifting, ethical attitudes to war and peace, too.

Importantly, not only the just war theory (or more generally the claim to justify killing innocents when necessary) but pacifism, too (understood as the rejection of any war, or even any violence, as morally impermissible), can be argued to be implicitly theodicist. This is because the pacifist is willing to sacrifice, in the interest of their own moral purity, the innocent victims of oppression that must not, according to the pacifist, be defended by waging war against the oppressor.[26] It is just a different kind of sacrifice, irreducible to the sacrificing of innocents due to waging war. We should not, then, be tempted by either easy pacifism or naïve beliefs in the justifiability of war. Only a narrow critical path between these extremes is open for the antitheodicist thinker committed to recognizing the reality of others' meaningless suffering. The availability of this critical ethical stance toward both pacifism and the just war theory depends on antitheodicism, that is, on the ethical necessity of taking others' suffering seriously in the sense of not interpreting it in terms of any overarching teleological scheme of meaningfulness – either

---

26 Again, this criticism primarily targets absolute, non-negotiable pacifism, instead of broader construals of pacifism as an ethical and social theory promoting peaceful and non-violent values (cf. Fiala 2010, 2018).

religious or secular. With these tentative conclusions drawn from our case study, and from our critical discussion (earlier in this chapter) of secular theodicies sketching a kind of research program for the antitheodicist today, we may turn to more fundamental questions of what is at stake, ethically, in the theodicism versus antitheodicism debate.

Chapter 5

ANTITHEODICY AND ETHICAL SERIOUSNESS

The discourse on antitheodicy introduced in the previous chapters is essentially ethically motivated. There is, as various antitheodicists from the early modern period to the present have argued, something seriously wrong – ethically wrong – in the theodicist picture according to which suffering must receive an overarching meaning or purpose from an absolute divine perspective (or a secular variant, such as some kind of teleological structure of history or a presupposed political ideology). Antitheodicism therefore joins Mara van der Lugt's (2021, 3) "dark" thinking and hopeful pessimism in sharing her "concern over how to speak truthfully, meaningfully, and compassionately about human […] suffering" (see also van der Lugt 2025). As has become clear, I do not mean that antitheodicism would necessarily have to endorse van der Lugt's defense of pessimism, however, because antitheodicism in my broadly pragmatist articulation is committed to meliorism rather than pessimism (see below, as well as the discussion of pragmatist antitheodicy in Chapter 3). It is nevertheless crucial for such meliorist antitheodicism to take seriously the lessons of pessimism, and one of the questions emerging here is the very possibility of meliorism as a coherent middle-ground option between optimism and pessimism.

In its own peculiar way, antitheodicism, while criticizing illusory meaning-making, tries to make sense of suffering in its meaninglessness. This is a thoroughly ethical project – or so I am trying to further show in this chapter also hopefully deepening our sense of what the meaning of the ethical amounts to here. The purpose of this rather substantial chapter is thus to enhance our understanding of what exactly it means to say that theodicies ought to be rejected for ethical reasons. In particular, I hope to explain why ethical antitheodicism should not be conceived of as a moralizing project but, rather, as a broadly Kantian project of locating the necessary conditions for the possibility of our so much as having an ethical stance at all in the rejection of the theodicist project of justifying or excusing suffering (a project to which, recall, also atheist critics of theodicy are committed simply by presupposing the expectation of theodicy as a premise in their argument against theism). In this sense, the present chapter continues to further articulate the historical antitheodicisms briefly introduced in Chapter 3, many of which can be claimed to incorporate a transcendental dimension – in some cases *pace* their authors' own self-understanding. Accordingly, we will take a step onto a philosophical – indeed, transcendental – meta-level in this chapter, also adding depth to the treatment of contemporary secular examples of theodicy versus antitheodicy discussed in the previous chapter and the kind of questions that need to be pursued when this general significance of the theodicy discourse is taken seriously. We should not forget the pragmatist message that even the most theoretical examination of antitheodicism is designed to be relevant to such practical concerns.[1] The fundamental ethical seriousness of antitheodicism lies not as much in its transcendental depths as in its practical real-life significance – or, rather, in the realization that there is no principled theory versus practice dichotomy to be drawn in the first place.

5.1. Humanism

We should begin exploring the ethical seriousness of antitheodicism by discussing the *proper focus* of the theodicy versus antitheodicy debate. Traditionally, recall, theodicies (and "defenses") are put forward within the theism versus atheism debate, considering the moral reasons that God (or, again, some metaphysical secular proxy, like historical teleology) might have for allowing suffering. The attempt is made to view the problem of evil and suffering from a God's-Eye View, as it were, to the extent that this is possible for finite beings like us. In contrast, ever since Kant's ethical turn in the theodicy discussion, the antitheodicist insists on viewing the problem from our limited human perspectives.

We can see how this contrast becomes relevant by considering a recent objection to moral antitheodicies. James Franklin (2020) compares theodicies regarding their alleged moral "offensiveness," and he (in my view) rightly rejects some standard theodicies, such as those appealing to free will or "soul-making," agreeing with antitheodicists that such appeals may indeed be considered morally offensive as they disregard the full significance of the victims'

---

[1] Recall the basic pragmatist idea guiding this entire inquiry: there is no theory versus practice dichotomy to be reasonably drawn here. I will return to this point in more detail.

suffering.[2] However, he argues that the "best possible world" theodicy derived from Leibniz (claiming that an omniscient and omnipotent absolutely good God could not possibly have created any other world) escapes such considerations of moral offensiveness. God can be excused simply because he did not have a real choice in creating any better world than the one he did create. The Leibnizian theodicy is compatible with the fact that there is a lot of evil and suffering in the world; this only has to be recognized as necessary for the whole, as the world *in toto* could not be any better than it is. Thus, Franklin says, "the Leibnizian theory does not assert anything about the overall goodness of the world except that it exceeds some bar that makes its creation better than nothing" (ibid., 570).

Now, attempting to imagine how things look from God's perspective, Franklin notes that "choosing the absolutely best world one can create is necessarily morally unimpeachable. If any other world had been chosen, God would be open to criticism as permitting more evil than the minimum" (ibid.). God is defended here on the grounds that he could not have done any better. The problem in Franklin's argument, from an antitheodicist standpoint, is precisely this attempt to reach out to the divine perspective, which amounts to making theodicist assumptions right at the beginning. Antitheodicism, in the sense I am introducing it in this book, is a deeply *humanistic* endeavor in maintaining that the truly serious issue we face when considering theodicies and antitheodicies is not the moral standing of God's choices (about which we can know nothing, as Kant, among others, taught us – and as Job already learned in failing to get a proper response from God that would have justified innocent suffering) but, simply, our engagement with others' suffering.

---

2 I am here considering Franklin's argument only as a recent example. On the limitations of moral antitheodicy arguments that in one way or another claim theodicies to yield a *"proxy* endorsement for horrendous evil," see also, e.g., Simpson 2009 (for this phrase, see 158). Simpson classifies these arguments into three main categories: arguments "from insensitivity," "from detachment," and "from harmful consequences" (such as legitimizing oppressive social structures). It seems to me that Simpson, by treating antitheodicies as straightforwardly moral (or even moralizing), does not appreciate the transcendental status of antitheodicism (to be explored further in this chapter). For an exchange on the differences between moral and conceptual antitheodicies, see again Snellman 2019 and Berenson 2019. Echazú (2024a) insightfully argues that both Simpson's (2009) and Snellman's (2019) arguments against moral antitheodicy are flawed attempts to show the question-begging character of moral antitheodicy. Simpson, in particular, confuses criticisms of theodicy within the theodicy framework and antitheodicies presented as criticisms of that framework itself. It is easy to agree with this analysis.

Franklin compares God's situation in creating the world to the thought experiment popularly known as the "trolley problem." Imagine a trolley running loose and killing five people if nothing is done, and imagine further that you can switch the gear causing the trolley to turn to another track and thus to kill only one person. Should you do this, actively choosing to kill one (instead of letting five die) in order to minimize the damage? In creating, God has an analogous trolley problem, according to Franklin: "Among the scenarios facing him, he must choose the best one. If he does choose the best – as the Leibnizian claims – then it is not appropriate to criticize him morally" (ibid., 571). Franklin goes on to criticize antitheodicists for having offered an irrelevant moral charge against God by not construing the situation in terms of a trolley problem.

While Franklin's argument may seem plausible as a defense of the way in which the Leibnizian theodicist views God's situation, this, in my view, is precisely the wrong approach to the general issue of gratuitous suffering (as should be clear after the discussion of secular theodicies in the previous chapter). What is crucial in the antitheodicist charge is *not* moral criticism of God's choices or God's moral standing; they are inevitably – and, if God exists, rather obviously – beyond our epistemic and ethical evaluation. It makes little sense to say that we humans could genuinely assess God's actions (if we believe in God – and it makes even less sense if we don't). What we are assessing, of course, are human beings' moral reactions and responses, our own and others'. The claim to examine God's moral situation is seriously misleading in turning our attention away from the crucial ethical issues pertaining to the ways in which we speak and reason about suffering. What is at issue in the theodicy versus antitheodicy discussion is *our* inescapably human ethical engagement with reality, especially with others' suffering, not God's (real or imagined) moral standing in creating the world. Whatever moral criticism the antitheodicist presents, that criticism is directed against human beings – us, or the views we hold and the thoughts we think – and not against God, no matter whether the antitheodicist believes in God or not. This is another way of saying (as I have done earlier) that the theodicism versus antitheodicism issue is ethically more fundamental than the theism versus atheism one.[3] Antitheodicism is, essentially, humanism.

Accordingly, antitheodicism ought to be seen as a thoroughly *human* project whose critique is targeted not at a metaphysically postulated divinity but

---

[3] For a more detailed exposition of all the obvious mistakes in Franklin's argument (including his crude misreading of the antitheodicism defended in Kivistö and Pihlström 2016), see Pihlström 2023, 143–146.

at us, at human beings whose attitudes to their fellows' (as well as non-human beings') sufferings can be argued to be ethically problematic if phrased in terms of theodicist speculation or even in terms of a mere expectation of such speculation to be delivered. Moreover, this antitheodicist ethical critique should above all focus on *ourselves*, on our own theodicist tendencies in explicitly or implicitly justifying or excusing suffering with reference to some comprehensive "good" it may bring about, or our instrumentalizing suffering in the service of yielding such goods, including (at an abstract level) the "good" of finding the world comprehensible.[4] The ethical critique inherent in antitheodicism challenges this very pursuit of comprehensibility if it runs counter to our need to recognize others' suffering for what it is.

Whether or not God exists, we humans are responsible for the ways in which we conceptualize and engage with the evil and suffering *we* perceive in the world. If God does exist, then he is *per definitionem* utterly superior to us, not subject to our moral evaluation; God does as he wishes, as emphasized in God's speech to Job, which provides no response to Job's demand for justice but basically offers a catalogue of the majesties of the divine creation. A theodicist logic might be morally acceptable from a divine perspective, but this is not an issue for us, as we have no ways of judging the criteria of such acceptability. Our problem is, and remains, human. The contrast between theodicism and antitheodicism can thus also be compared to the one between a theocentrist and an anthropocentrist way of viewing the world (again, without confusing these with theism and atheism). Analogously, in van der Lugt's (2021, 95) terms, early modern philosophers' optimism (theodicy) takes a cosmic perspective, while pessimism (antitheodicy) – just as, I would like to add, meliorism – considers "the *creaturely* perspective" as primary or even as the only relevant perspective regarding the issue of creaturely suffering (ibid., 102). On the other hand, *anthropocentrism* – understood here as the inescapable humanist idea that we only have our human perspectives for examining any moral issues, including evil and suffering – must be carefully distinguished from any illusory *anthropomorphism*, which is actually one of the major sources of confusion in the theodicist tradition (cf. Schönbaumsfeld 2018, 2021). It is precisely, or at least largely, because we have a tendency of comparing God to a human moral agent that we arrive at theodicies, including the assumption

---

4 See again Neiman 2002 and Snellman 2023 for discussions of evil as yielding a general problem of comprehensibility (cf. also Nagasawa 2024).

that we could judge, and excuse, God's moral standing based on a comparison to a thought experiment like the trolley problem.[5]

Note also that emphasizing the humanism of antitheodicism by no means entails that the moral critique inherent in antitheodicism would have to ignore the suffering of non-human beings. While the problem of animal suffering is, unsurprisingly, often approached in terms of theodicies or "defenses" among philosophers of religion, even those rejecting typical traditional theodicies (e.g., van Inwagen 2006, Chapter 7; Sollereder 2019; Keltz 2025), the antitheodicist approach questions any appeals to the actual or possible meaningfulness of suffering in this context as firmly as it does in the context of human suffering. However, this critique must, again, be understood as a human project. It is only from within a human perspective that we can evaluate our moral practices of dealing with animals and their suffering, and of conceptualizing that suffering in philosophical or theoretical discourse. It should be clear to us all, I believe, that developing an ethically more sustainable relationship to animals and non-human nature generally is one of the key ethical challenges we face in our time, but it is compatible with this recognition to maintain that human beings crucially differ from any animals we are familiar with in the sense of living – for better and worse – in a normatively structured world of meanings and moral problems.

As Raimond Gaita (2004 [1991], 117) aptly puts it, an animal can suffer enormously but it would make no sense whatsoever – for us humans – to say that an animal could, like Job, "curse the day it was born." Any antitheodicist approach to animal suffering must therefore appreciate the fundamentally humanistic character of antitheodicism that attributes the possibility of suffering going indefinitely deep only to human beings (see Gaita 2000, 239).[6] We may say, simplifying somewhat, that while ordinary humanistic

---

5   It might also be suggested that theodicies, rather than antitheodicies, tend to view the world anthropocentrically in the sense of expecting that suffering out to make sense for us humans. See Clement's (2020) analysis of Milton's *Paradise Lost* and the God of the *Book of Job* in this regard. While the world is not to be expected to have been "made for humans" (as in anthropocentrism of the problematic theodicist kind analyzed by Clement), our response to the frustration of such expectations can only be a moral evaluation of, and within, our human standpoint.

6   For an antitheodicist examination of the problem of animal suffering raising these issues about human exceptionalism, see Pihlström 2025, Chapter 3, with particular reference to Gaita's (2000, 2004 [1991]) view that it only makes sense (for us) to say that human beings, not animals, have "souls" in a moral or spiritual sense of the concept of a soul that avoids metaphysical speculation about what souls "are" and which entities possess them. (Keltz 2025 contains a variety of other perspectives on the problem of animal suffering.)

antheodicies emphasize the (possible) meaninglessness of suffering, refusing to accept theodicist claims to meaning, an antitheodicism directed at the problem of animal suffering, based on such humanism, argues instead that in the case of animals there is no scale of meaningfulness versus meaninglessness at all in the sense in which we may find such a scale in the case of human lives.

5.2. Theory and Practice

Chapter 3 introduced, among historical sources of antitheodicism, pragmatism, especially its Jamesian variant. While this book cannot explore pragmatism in detail, it is informed by the pragmatist idea that we should not approach the theodicy versus antitheodicy issue by assuming any dichotomy between the theoretical and the practical. This dichotomy is often invoked by theodicists when they encounter the moral charge of neglecting the full reality of the victims' suffering. When that point in the debate is reached, the theodicist typically reminds their opponent that what they are doing is merely trying to solve a theoretical puzzle. The rejection of any such easy theoretical versus practical dualisms is an important dimension of the morally serious attitude to suffering that antitheodicism insists on. Far from simply maintaining that the practical (ethical, existential) dimensions of the problem are primary to the theoretical (intellectual) ones, the pragmatist antitheodicist criticizes attempts to operate in terms of that dichotomy in the first place.

In many cases, theodicists, including those pursuing a "defense," rely on such a dichotomy between theory and practice by admitting that at a purely theoretical level their justifications for evil and suffering may indeed fail to adequately acknowledge the suffering other, or the other's experiences of meaningless suffering, while also maintaining that this is not a philosophically or ethically dramatic failure, because the problem itself, at least in its core form, *is* highly theoretical, to be distinguished from the practical task of consolation or (in more explicitly theological contexts) pastoral care. The theodicist may even admit that when actually faced by the suffering other, they should not engage in theorization about evil and theodicies but offer practical consolation to the sufferer. For example, Peter van Inwagen (2006, 12) notes that his philosophical examination of the problem of evil *is* "purely intellectual" and that his "defense," shifting the burden of proof to the atheist, is not intended to comfort anyone, even hypothetically (ibid., 108). It would then seem that the practical need to acknowledge the victim of suffering is not neglected but simply distinguished from the theoretical project of theodicies.

It can be argued, however, that it is the very attempt to defend theodicism by drawing a sharp theory versus practice dualism that itself, at a meta-level, constitutes an ethical failure of acknowledging the other. We may imagine this type of argument being developed from a pragmatist perspective, in particular. The appropriate way to ethically recognize the suffering other and the meaninglessness of their suffering is precisely to avoid drawing such a dichotomy at all, even at a meta-level – that is, to avoid engaging in an allegedly purely theoretical argumentative exchange of mere intellectual ideas to be brought into the discussion for and against theodicies, or to view the practical problem of evil and suffering simply as something to which such theoretical ideas can be applied. The issue, as emphasized by the antitheodicist, concerns the ways in which our practical contexts of responding to suffering may and should constrain our theorization about the problem of evil and suffering right from the beginning. The dichotomy-drawing itself is vulnerable to this ethical critique. While the historical (or recent) antitheodicists explored in Chapter 3 usually do not put the matter in so many words, it seems that something like this argument is common to thinkers as diverse as James, Levinas, and Wittgensteinians like Phillips. In this sense, I believe it is fair to treat pragmatism as a kind of meta-theory for antitheodicist reflection more broadly: it is essential for antitheodicism as an ethical critique of the theodicist tendency to fail to recognize others' suffering to reject easy appeals to a dualism between the theoretical and the practical. The theoretical *is* always already the practical – at least for beings like us.[7]

5.3. The Return of Theodicies?

It might seem that the arguments presented earlier in this book – many of them found in historical classics of the antitheodicist framework – should, if they are compelling (as I think they are), be taken to have refuted theodicies and theodicism for good. However, we should not celebrate a victory over theodicies too quickly, as theodicies also seem to have a tendency to always come back in a different form, being virtually impossible to entirely avoid (cf. Pihlström 2021, Chapter 6). It remains to be examined whether even an ethically motivated antitheodicist rearticulation of ideas such as God and morality – all the way from Kant to more recent antitheodicists – might in the end amount to something like "theodicy by other means."

For example, it may be asked whether philosophers like William James and Hans Jonas, when "rethinking" the concept of God in terms of finitude,

---

7 This argument would have to be backed up with references to the pragmatist tradition. Here, as this is no study of pragmatism as such, I can only refer the reader to some of my earlier work on the topic, e.g., Pihlström 2020a, 2021, and 2023.

processuality, and limitation, revising the metaphysics of the divinity to meet our ethical need to recognize meaningless suffering, ultimately seek to offer a harmonious picture motivated by a "temptation" to theodicy (cf. Bernstein 2002) that can never be silenced for good. Our need to render suffering a meaningful element of our world-picture – at the antitheodicist meta-level, even if not in terms of first-order theodicies – is a natural, presumably inescapable human need. This yields a kind of "dialectics of antitheodicism": even the best-meaning antitheodicies may be implicitly quasi-theodicist in ultimately seeking to harmonize our views on suffering, morality, and God (or some secular alternative). Even though acknowledging the (at least potential) meaninglessness of suffering challenges any alleged theodicist harmony or reconciliation, it is precisely this acknowledgment itself that may, at the meta-level, seem like a harmonious way of being ultimately reconciled with our world of suffering, as the reconciliatory pursuit is itself finally liberated from the theodicist confusions that only increase suffering by claiming it to be meaningful. Ivan's handing back the ticket would then itself be an act of reconciliation precisely by being a gesture of non-reconciliation.

Moreover, theodicies may seem to return just when we had believed to be able to leave them behind. The "temptation to theodicy" identified and criticized by (among others) Levinas and Bernstein is thus more complex than it initially seems, because even antitheodicism is not immune to this temptation. It is like the ineradicable inclination of "radical evil" in human beings – to put the matter analogously to Kant's theory of radical evil. Levinas, one of the most important antitheodicists (see Chapter 3), spoke of the implicit theodicy of Western philosophy, and this, troublingly, extends to antitheodicism, too, possibly even his own.

Even Kant, to whom I have historically traced the entire antitheodicist tradition, may seem to have posited a theodicy by other means in his account of the "highest good" (*summum bonum*), that is, the (in his view) legitimate hope that the harmony of moral duty or virtue and happiness may eventually be secured by God through an "infinite progression" of our existence as immortal souls. The postulates of practical reason, including God's existence and the immortality of the soul,[8] are of course practical, not theoretical, and we cannot know anything about their truth or reality; in this sense, Kant's critical philosophy steers clear from any theodicist claim to know that harmony will at the end of the day be achieved, or that apparent "counterpurposiveness" (in the language of the "Theodicy Essay") will be reconciled with God's

---

8 For Kant's doctrine of the postulates, see the Dialectic of *Kritik der praktischen Vernunft* (1788), available in Kant 1983.

creation. Yet, the postulation of God's existence and immortality is ethically unavoidable for us, because otherwise we could not be coherently committed to pursuing what the moral law (the categorical imperative) absolutely commands us to pursue. ("Ought" implies "can".) Although Kant firmly rejected all theoretical theodicies, his antitheodicism seems to allow for the possibility of a harmony – postulated, not known or even knowable – that finally serves the same practical end as a theodicy might serve. I am not claiming that this is exactly how we ought to read Kant, but I believe we ought to identify a worry here, possibly troubling his antitheodicist project from within.[9]

Among the philosophers that I have classified as (quasi-)Kantian antitheodicists, James also seems to be vulnerable to the charge that, despite his antitheodicism, he lets theodicies slip back in. We saw in Chapter 3 that he rejected both Leibnizian and Hegelian theodicies allegedly rendering evil and suffering purposive. Urging us to adopt a morally "strenuous mood" in struggling against evil is part and parcel of his pragmatic meliorism. However, as is well known, James had his mysticist moments and carefully analyzed the nature of mystical experience (see especially James 1958 [1902]). Like Kant in his doctrine of the "highest good," James seems to grant us the right to believe that everything will or at least may ultimately end up in a mystical harmony, even if his general pragmatist approach denies the legitimacy of such a "moral holiday," as he calls it in *Pragmatism* (1975 [1907], Lecture III). At least if the potential religious believer has a moral inclination toward mystical faith, postulating eventual harmony, such beliefs seem to be licensed according to James's "will to believe" strategy (see James 1979 [1897]).[10] If theodicist (mystical) harmony meets our ethical, existential, and religious needs, and there is no obvious evidence against it, then the Jamesian pragmatist may find it justified for an individual to believe in such harmony, after all. At least the possibility of theodicies is kept open even if the will to believe method is formulated as an element of a pragmatist approach that is itself (as I claimed in Chapter 3) framed by a serious consideration of the reality of evil.

---

9 Another way of putting the matter is to say that Kant's critical engagement with theodicies in the "Theodicy Essay" is self-critical not only in the sense that Kant rejects the (particularly Leibnizian) theodicies he was inclined to accept in his pre-critical period but also in the sense that he examines the kind of theodicist views he himself still held in the 1780s in his ethical writings, especially in the form of the postulates. See van der Lugt 2021, Chapter 7. (On these grounds, van der Lugt is right to point out that we should not simply read Kant as an antitheodicist. Here I basically agree, though I still think we can trace the antitheodicist tradition back to Kant's ideas.)

10 I have discussed James's views in this regard at considerable length elsewhere (e.g., Pihlström 2021, Chapter 4), so here I just leave the matter at this.

A particularly explicit endorsement of ethico-religious harmony takes place in Wittgenstein's philosophy, even though "Wittgensteinian" antitheodicism can be identified as one of the main options in the antitheodicist framework. We noted in Chapter 3 that many Wittgensteinian thinkers (most prominently Phillips) reject theodicies as deep conceptual, moral, and religious confusions. Yet Wittgenstein himself may have thought otherwise. The pursuit of an ethical, metaphysical, or transcendental harmony in our relation to the world seems to be fundamental for the early Wittgenstein, in particular. Both in the *Tractatus* (Wittgenstein 1974 [1921]) and in the pre-Tractarian *Notebooks 1914-1916* (Wittgenstein 1961), we are told that happiness consists in a mystical kind of harmony with the world. While we might, if we are convinced by the kind of antitheodicist argumentation developed in this book, find acknowledging the meaninglessness and irreconcilability of suffering a necessary condition for seeing the world "rightly" (cf. Wittgenstein 1974 [1921], §6.54), this view itself, lucidly recognizing suffering for what it is, may at the meta-level be considered reconciliatory, yielding an ultimate harmony *sub specie aeternitatis* with the empirically disharmonious world. After all, the world of the "happy man" is, Wittgenstein famously wrote in the *Tractatus*, different from the world of the unhappy man (ibid., §6.43; see also Wittgenstein 1961, entry on July 29, 1916), and possibly an antitheodicist can be "happy" (at a meta-level even if not at the "first-order" level of being reconciled with the horrendous worldly facts of suffering) in the sense of having, with philosophical effort, achieved the "right" way of seeing the world. A harmonious overall perspective on suffering, albeit an antitheodicist one, is then once again offered, and this could be regarded as a return of theodicy in the guise of antitheodicy.

Possibly, even Levinas's uncompromising antitheodicism may end up bringing theodicies back (and he might have admitted that this inevitably happens, given our inclination to follow the theodicist temptation that has made theodicism implicit in Western philosophy in general), because the recognition of the utter uselessness of suffering and the naked meaninglessness of evil violating the vulnerable other is, again, at the meta-level, reconciliatory. Here, finally, we are able to view the world harmoniously as what it is: a call to infinite ethical responsibility to and for the other human being. As soon as we realize this (and as soon as we have read enough Levinas, someone might sarcastically add), we can finally relax and accept our infinitely demanding ethical predicament, provided that we never forget the impossibility of facing the other human being as sincerely as we ought to.

The key point in antitheodicism, however, is that no such relaxation is possible – ever. At least it is never fully or completely possible. Ethics is, indeed, *infinitely demanding* (cf. Critchley 2010). Even Levinas may not be free from the tendency toward theodicy (any more than any other antitheodicist is), but we also find in his work resources for taking the necessary steps of liberation from this tendency. Qua antitheodicists, we should continuously struggle against any naïve acceptance even of the meta-level picture of harmonious meaningfulness that would seem to be available to us as soon as we have embraced antitheodicism. This embrace does not yield any moral holiday, at any point.[11] Nor should antitheodicism, then, ever be reduced to a final complete picture of the way things are (e.g., in terms of metaphysical realism allegedly offering a view from a transcendent vantage point). On the contrary, *this* temptation should be constantly countered by continuously refocusing on the potential absurdity of suffering.

Therefore, antitheodicism is, necessarily, an incomplete project. In a sense, "everything changes" – our entire way of viewing the world will be different – as soon as we reject theodicism. However, we should never rest satisfied with simply putting forward this antitheodicist stance as the final complete picture of how things are or the ultimate truth about our moral situation. We should, in brief, never turn antitheodicism itself into a totalizing, universally true, or metaphysically harmonious worldview. It is itself a position constantly in flux, and therefore an approach rather than any final theory. Even while claiming antitheodicism to be the only "true" or ethically acceptable choice, we should not be satisfied even with the antitheodicist perspective on the world of suffering. In general, the very notion of moral satisfaction is fundamentally challenged here. An antitheodicist attitude to suffering reminds us – constantly – that morality is an infinite task for us, and there is no way of ever completing this task in a satisfactory, or even decent, manner. Again, however, acknowledging *this* might seem to yield yet another quasi-theodicy, at an even higher meta-level. And so it goes, potentially indefinitely. The project of formulating a workable antitheodicy, or engaging in a consistently antitheodicist examination of the problem of suffering, is never completed but must constantly recognize its own tendencies of falling back into theodicist construals of meaning, reconciliation, and harmony.

Along with the acknowledgment of the possibility that theodicies may always return, we should acknowledge another significant limitation to our antitheodicist pursuits, namely, what I like to call the impossibility of full acknowledgment.[12] This is a crucial aspect of our recognizing the other as genuinely other, someone whose experiences of suffering (or anything) cannot

---

11 Note that this formulation, in a sense, integrates Levinasian and Jamesian antitheodicisms.
12 See Kivistö and Pihlström 2016, Chapter 6, for some discussion of this reflexive issue.

be reduced to *our* meaning-making conceptualizations of what those sufferings ultimately amount to from an overarching metaphysical perspective. The impossibility of ever fully acknowledging the entire truth about the suffering of any individual – such as an individual moral witness of a historical atrocity – is a major element of the antitheodicist acknowledgment of others' suffering generally. This is to make the familiar point that our relation to others is not primarily one of knowing but of acknowledging (cf. Cavell 1979). In this case, what we must, and can only, acknowledge is that another "soul" is in pain – adopting an "attitude towards a soul" along Wittgensteinian lines – without claiming to know that the other "has" a soul, conceived of as a metaphysical entity.[13]

5.4. Antitheodicy and Historical Understanding

Examples of irreconcilable suffering are very often drawn from history, based on historical research. Human history as we know it is an inexhaustible source of horrendous evil, and therefore historical understanding plays a fundamental role in our reflections on what is at stake in ethics (see Little 2022). The project of antitheodicy is thus centrally related to our conceptions of the nature of history and historiography. This should not be surprising, of course, given the central status of events such as the Holocaust – a historical event that according to many scholars changed our entire moral world – as something that antitheodicists seek to respond to (to the extent that the term "antitheodicy" was coined, as we recall, by Braiterman in response to the Holocaust).

An example of what might be described as a pragmatist meliorist ethical constraint on historiography could be the need to avoid teleological accounts of history allegedly rendering historical events, especially sufferings, "meaningful" in some ultimate metaphysical sense. In particular, such accounts could rely on explicit or implicit (often secular) theodicies claiming to make historical crises and sufferings meaningful or purposive from a transcendent perspective unavailable to the protagonists of historical events themselves. Admittedly, the historian, relying on empirical evidence, typically constructs interpretations and explanations attributing a kind of "meaningfulness" as well as causal connections to the events studied, but it may be argued that such interpretations should not – for ethical reasons – be grounded in, nor entail, teleological (e.g., theodicist, or metaphysically optimist – nor pessimist,

---

13 For Wittgenstein's reflections on having an "attitude towards a soul" (*eine Einstellung zur Seele*), see Wittgenstein 1953, Part II, iv; cf. Gaita 2004 [1991], Chapter 10.

for that matter) accounts of overall historical meaningfulness (or lack thereof) that would be presupposed prior to empirical inquiry. Maintaining a critical distance to such metaphysical accounts of history, while also maintaining an ordinary empirical realism about historical facts and events, pragmatist philosophy of historiography – and more generally pragmatist philosophy of the humanities (cf. Pihlström 2022) – can offer conceptual and methodological resources for critically investigating the ways in which such broadly ethical constraints can be taken to be relevant to historiographical (and other humanistic) scholarship. While *philosophy of historiography* must be carefully distinguished from traditional metaphysical *philosophy of history* (e.g., speculations about historical progress), ethical insights drawn from the latter, particularly non-teleological and antitheodicist meliorism, can also crucially inform the former.

Accordingly, the pragmatist meliorist may argue that while deepening our awareness of history should (in a broad sense) serve ("ameliorate") human life, our lives are not appropriately "served" by subordinating them to teleological or theodicist quasi-explanations of ultimate metaphysical meaningfulness presupposing transcendent non-human or superhuman purposiveness underlying contingent historical processes. Taking this ethical constraint seriously, we should also explore ways of integrating pragmatist meliorism with a moderate realism about the ontology and epistemology of humanistic (specifically historiographical) research that views historical scholarship as a genuinely cognitive enterprise – a rational, empirically responsible pursuit of truth – despite its arguably inevitable ethical value-ladenness. Insofar as meliorism, carefully distinguished from both optimism and pessimism, is considered a value commitment guiding humanistic research, we must view all truth-seeking and thus even the ontology of historical inquiry in an irreducibly ethical context. It can be argued that historians' (often implicit) ethical value choices and background assumptions play a role in the ways in which historical truths are discovered and even in acknowledging the reality of historical facts and events, especially ethically significant crises and disruptions, such as the Holocaust and other horrors motivating an antitheodicist approach to the study of history. Thus, even the historical past is ontologically dependent on our ethically constrained practices of knowing and understanding the world in terms of our future-oriented practices of living in the world within which we are challenged to do what we can to alleviate suffering, although this view must not be interpreted in terms of an antirealism that would make the past itself (absurdly) causally or empirically depend on our contingent attitudes or cognitive states.

Therefore, while there is, we may argue, a sense in which antitheodicism and meliorism play not only an *ethically* guiding or constraining role in historians' practices of research but even an *ontologically* significant role in (co-)constituting the historical reality investigated and interpreted (cf. Pihlström 2025, Chapter 2), philosophers of historiography are challenged to make sure that recognizing this ontological relevance of ethical constraints does not lead to a slippery slope toward full-blown antirealism, according to which historical reality would simply be "constructed" by the historian. Antitheodicism presupposes historical realism, at least to the extent that historical crises and sufferings are acknowledged as fully real. Meliorism can thus be regarded as one aspect of (for example) a pragmatist pursuit of a critical middle ground between metaphysically realist accounts of "ready-made" teleologically pre-structured (historical) reality captured in a theodicist narrative, on the one hand, and relativist or antirealist views according to which there is no shared objective reality to be investigated at all, on the other. This parallels the way in which meliorism functions, according to Jamesian pragmatism, as a middle path between optimism and pessimism (see Chapter 3 as well as Section 5.6). Meliorism, however, should only be understood (here) as a constraint on our historiographical pursuits of truth, not a pre-given metaphysical account to which history needs to conform.

The kind of historical realism worth defending, it may be argued, is a (Kantian-like) empirical realism subordinated to (what we may call) transcendental pragmatism, which views postulations of historical facts and events, qua value-laden, as constitutively dependent on an ethically grounded non-teleological account of history. It is, in other words, not just another contingent historical fact among others that history is not teleologically structured; this is a constitutive, albeit practice-embedded, condition for the possibility of historical ontology, ethically conceived.[14] As a constraint on historical ontology, antitheodicist non-teleological meliorism plays a pragmatic-cum-transcendental role in rendering historical reality a possible object of investigation.

The need to develop our understanding of history, including the philosophy of historiography (including even our ontology of historiography), in an antitheodicist manner can thus be concretized in the requirement that historical narrative must not be teleological or quasi-theodicist but must appropriately acknowledge contingency and contingent suffering. The non-teleological account of historical events extends, in principle, to both personal (individual) life histories and general historical events, including world

---

14 Specifically, for the antitheodicist, it is not just a contingent fact of the matter that the Holocaust does not have any theodicist or teleological "meaning" or "purpose"; it is constitutive of our understanding of the Holocaust as the historical event it is that we do not ascribe such meaning or purpose into the event.

history, even though we should also be careful to avoid simply telling others that their personal histories lack the kind of meanings they themselves might associate with their lives. Neither theodicy nor antitheodicy should be imposed on others, or their histories, from the outside.

5.5. The Monstrosity of the Idea of Providence

We may here consider a personal case potentially illustrating antitheodicism regarding history generally. Primo Levi, one of the most important and arguably ethically the most compelling writers to emerge from among Holocaust survivors, did not explicitly thematize theodicy or antitheodicy in his work, but his writings about the Holocaust can clearly be interpreted within the antitheodicist framework, arguing that we should not infest the horrible historical events with any justificatory meanings. In particular, Levi is absolutely clear in rejecting – with horror – any idea of providence, emphasizing, in contrast, the contingency and sheer chance in survival (see, e.g., Levi 1988 [1986], 117; 1996 [1958], 157–158).[15] After the Holocaust, we cannot possibly continue to use the concept of providence (non-ironically); or better, after the Holocaust, we see that this was *never* possible. Levi would be horrified by, say, apologetic Christian philosophers' theodicist attempts to postulate some possible meaning in the Holocaust, or by defenses of a postmortem reconciliation in terms of some divine compensation theodicy (cf., e.g., Adams 1999). Even the more secular idea that Levi himself would have been somehow "destined" to survive in order to be able to write his books "seemed monstrous" to him, because those who did survive ("the saved") were not at all the best but only "the fittest," and in some ways they were even the worst (Levi 1988 [1986], 62–63; cf. Agamben 2002 [1999], 60), which is to say that, ironically, *they* were "the drowned" rather than "the saved," after all. Levi writes:

> My religious friend had told me that I survived so that I could bear witness. I have done so, as best I could, [...] but the thought that this testifying of mine could by itself gain for me the privilege of surviving [...] troubles me, because I cannot see any proportion between the privilege and its outcome. (Levi 1988 [1986], 63; cf. 143.)

This remark may (non-anachronistically) be read in the context of Levinas's (2006 [1982], 97) previously discussed comment on the disproportionality of Holocaust suffering in comparison to any possible theodicy, explicit or

---

15 This aspect of Levi's thinking has been discussed by various commentators, including Alford (2009, 143).

implicit. Nothing whatsoever, nothing in the entire world, could be so good or valuable that it might render the Holocaust acceptable, justified, or excusable in any humanly understandable sense. Discussing Levi's reading of the *Book of Job*, C. Fred Alford (2009, 101) perceptively points out that, for Levi, even to *ask* the theodicy question, "Why do the innocent suffer if God is all good and all powerful?", is to misunderstand "one's place in the universe."[16] In our terms, this is to reject the theodicist approach altogether.

Accordingly, Levi can be interpreted as an antitheodicist who found it problematic (to put it mildly) to ask theodicy-driven questions at all – even though, with the kind of irony that only a literary work allows us, it is actually a Nazi guard who tells him, "There is no 'why' here" (*Hier gibt's kein warum*) (see Levi 1996 [1958]). It is this painful lesson we must learn from the Nazi assault on humanity – of course learning that it is not unique to Nazism or the Holocaust but extends to the overall human condition.

Levi tells us that only once during his imprisonment, facing a "selection" (and thus imminent mortal danger), did he feel a temptation to pray – which he rejected: "A prayer under these conditions would have been not only absurd (what rights could I claim? and from whom?) but blasphemous, laden with the greatest impiety of which a non-believer is capable" (Levi 1988 [1986], 118).[17] His account of what happened after another selection at Auschwitz in 1944 is also relevant to antitheodicism more broadly precisely because it characterizes what he found a deeply blasphemous prayer. In *If This Is a Man* (1996 [1958]), Levi describes a case in which an Auschwitz prisoner named Kuhn

---

16 Levi's own non-religiosity need not prevent antitheodicists with a Christian or theistic background from employing his analysis of the Nazis' utter degradation of their victims through entirely useless violence for the purposes of their antitheodicy arguments: see, e.g., Roth 2004, especially 282–283. Generally, the Holocaust is as important as a historical source of experience making antitheodicism almost a necessity for theist antitheodicists as it is for atheist ones. We should avoid the (in itself theodicist) tendency to view the Holocaust as a piece of evidence against theism (or against any religious position), though we may fully understand those who did or do lose their religious faith through contemplating the historical reality of the Holocaust. Even though antitheodicism is compatible with a religious outlook on life, historical disruptions such as the Holocaust do remind us that this compatibility may not be easy to maintain.

17 Levi (1988 [1986], 118) says that he was not religious when entering Auschwitz and that he thought that it would have been wrong for him to "change the rules of the game at the end of the match." Thus, obviously, his Holocaust experience did not feed into any argument from evil that would have concluded God's non-existence (see also the previous note). As Alfrod (2009, 146) notes, Levi "took seriously what he didn't believe."

was lucky to avoid a selection while a younger prisoner, Beppo, lying in the next bunk, was selected. Beppo, knowing that he would go to the gas chamber, had to listen to Kuhn praising God in a loud voice, thanking the divinity for saving him. Levi portrays Kuhn as a madman, finding his thankful prayer an obscene blasphemy: "Does Kuhn not understand that what happened today is an abomination, which no propitiatory prayer, no pardon, no expiation by the guilty – nothing at all in the power of man to do – can ever heal?" And he adds: "If I was God, I would spit at Kuhn's prayer" (ibid., 129–130).

Levi teaches us an extremely important lesson by discussing this special case. If we believe, like prisoner Kuhn, in a divinely just world-order even amid absurd horror, phrasing this in a loud prayer, we end up endorsing the fact that innocents are made to suffer and that this is somehow part of a rational, meaningful structure of historical teleology. Kuhn ultimately liberates the Nazis from their guilt, attributing final responsibility for the events to God. This is, essentially, what theodicies do, even if they also seek to exonerate God by speculating about his possible "good reasons" for choosing the particular world history he did choose. Therefore, Levi's Holocaust writings – and one culmination of them is, indeed, the Kuhn-Beppo scene – constitute an essential contribution to antitheodicism, showing us, repeatedly, that justifying others' pain is the source of all immorality (see again Levinas 2006 [1982], 85). As suggested in the previous section, understanding this must inform our understanding the nature of history, even the very ontology of historical events and processes, and the same goes for our personal encounters with historical events.[18]

It might even seem – extrapolating the case of Kuhn and Beppo – that *any* gratitude for what happened to me in my own life, for what I (or we) have received without my (our) own merit, is potentially at least implicitly

---

18 I am not claiming originality to an antitheodicist account of Levi. Jennifer L. Geddes (2018, §2) notes how outraged Levi is "at the theodical logic implicit in Kuhn's prayer." Not only does Kuhn fail to acknowledge Beppo, his fellow prisoner, but his failure is more general: "By ascribing responsibility to God for not being selected, Kuhn's prayer of thanks implicitly ascribes responsibility to God not only for Beppo's selection, but by extension, for the whole genocidal system" (ibid.). Invoking divine providence in this way is, Geddes agrees with Levi, blasphemous, and therefore "Levi's critique strikes to the heart of theodicy itself," directly comparing to Levinas's views on the uselessness of suffering (ibid., §§2–3). However, Geddes goes on to argue that just as we should not impose our theodicist account of the meaningfulness of suffering on a sufferer, conversely we should not impose our antitheodicism on someone who does believe in theodicies (ibid., §4). This is compatible with the suggestion – going through this volume – that antitheodicist critique is first and foremost a self-critical examination of our own temptation to theodicy.

theodicist.[19] By being grateful to God, or the world, or history, or whatever, for what there is and what there has been, I "accept" the world, no matter how unjust it is. Such acceptance could be taken to be theodicist to its core. It may also be self-deceptive and insincere, because by accepting the world I also accept horrendous injustice and pain.[20] Shouldn't the ethically decent thinker on the contrary morally reject such a disharmonious world we are living in, never agreeing to view history in the light of harmony, refusing any reconciliation like Dostoevsky's Ivan? Postulating harmony where there is none is what the character in Levi's story, prisoner Kuhn, does when thanking God in a high voice while fully aware of the utter disharmony of the world as experienced by Beppo who knows he has been selected to the gas. As Levi teaches us, nothing whatsoever could render this disharmony harmonious. No account of history, or God, could make it acceptable. Claiming it could be redeemed or that it serves some *telos* is, indeed, blasphemous. However, precisely by saying all *this* we may seem to "accept" it at a meta-level, after all – and thereby theodicies may again return to the picture, never to be silenced for good. We should learn that everything is not all right even after we have taken the antitheodicist turn and learned to view the world accordingly.

The dialectics of antitheodicist enlightenment (as we might call it) we identified earlier in this chapter (see Section 5.3) extends, then, to the picture of the ethical structure of history that (I have argued) seems to depend on our taking an antitheodicist stance on the world. We can never be certain that theodicies won't come back. Therefore, antitheodicism can only be *processual*. It is not as much a theory as a continuous pursuit of an antitheodicist understanding of the potential meaninglessness of suffering, conjoined with a realistic view of the radical evil of our notorious "will to meaning" that makes us unable to see others' suffering as what it is, without explaining it away as something that is in the end harmoniously reconcilable as meaningful. We can never completely liberate ourselves from this unethical tendency of theodicist harmonization, and therefore the process of antitheodicism needs

---

19 For comparison, see (again) van der Lugt's (2021, 65) account of Bayle's antitheodicy as a criticism of the (theodicist, optimist) idea that creatures should be grateful merely for their existence. The charge that creaturely complaint is ungrateful is, as van der Lugt puts it, "*the moral objection to anti-theodicy*" (ibid., 106; original emphasis). Accordingly, we should see the critical perspective on gratitude exemplified by Levi as an antitheodicist (moral) objection to theodicy coming relatively close to the kind of pessimist critique van der Lugt discusses.
20 Compare this, again, to Job's refusal to accept that what happened to him could have been just (see Chapter 3).

to be kept alive through continuous ethical vigilance, also pertaining to the ways in which we view our historical past as individuals and societies.

5.6. Pessimism, Meliorism, and Antinatalism

As Mara van der Lugt (2021, 2025) persuasively argues, sincere ethical thinking needs to be "dark" and "fragile" in the sense of taking pessimism seriously while not losing our capabilities of hope. As she writes: "At its best and deepest, what this kind of dark thinking, which is also a *fragile thinking*, achieves, is neither desperate nor passive nor fatalist: it is to open up new horizons of compassion and consolation" (van der Lugt 2021, 27). For many of us, for pragmatists in particular, it is more plausible to develop such "dark" yet possibly hopeful thinking in terms of meliorism than pessimism. However, we need to ask whether a *meliorist antitheodicy* – something that I am hoping to defend here – is really possible. Is antitheodicy, starting from the irreconcilability of meaningless suffering, inevitably committed to some form of pessimism, or can it avoid pessimism by advancing meliorism (as was in a sense assumed in the previous sections when I spoke of a meliorist pragmatist attitude to history and historiography)? At a certain extreme, this question leads us to consider whether rejecting theodicies entails embracing some form of extreme value-directed pessimism (in van der Lugt's vocabulary), for example, in the terms of contemporary ethical discourse, *antinatalism*, a radical view defended by, among others, David Benatar (2006) who argues that we would all be better off by not existing at all and that it is always wrong to bring new people (or, by extension, new creatures sensitive to pain and suffering) into existence.[21]

It is impossible here to engage in any full survey of the growing antinatalist discussion, even though it does bear clear resemblance to antitheodicy.

---

21 In particular, Benatar's antinatalism as an ethics of procreation is, in her view, comparable to Pierre Bayle's critical views on divine creation (see van der Lugt 2021, 58n78). I have criticized Benatar's antinatalism previously (Pihlström 2011, 2025), so I won't go into details here. Let me just note that this is one of the contexts in which the theodicy versus antitheodicy discussion is obviously relevant to more practical issues in applied ethics, including abortion and euthanasia. If one believes life to be so full of suffering that it would be better for us not to exist, it is also natural to maintain that abortion is (usually) permissible or even a duty (as Benatar holds). On the other hand, antitheodicism may lead to a completely different conclusion: there is no way in which we could attach a "price" to human life and its potential significance or insignificance – human beings, capable of suffering, are essentially priceless, incomparably precious (cf. Gaita 2004 [1991]) – and therefore abortion and euthanasia are examples of concrete moral problems that cannot be resolved at a general level but must always be examined in particular cases of personal urgency.

Superficially, antinatalism might be regarded as a version of antitheodicy: the reality of meaningless suffering is taken very seriously indeed, to the extent that this brute reality is claimed to render existence generally of negative rather than positive value. As van der Lugt (2021, e.g. 21) repeatedly points out, Benatar continues some of the arguments we already find in early modern critics of theodicy such as Pierre Bayle (see Chapter 3).[22] However, at a deeper level, I do not think that antinatalism is close to antitheodicism at all – not, at least, anywhere close to the brand of antitheodicism developed here. On the contrary, it treats suffering, and experiences of suffering, as "measurable" in a sense in which genuine antitheodicism does not. The "goods" and "harms" of life can, according to Benatar, be compared to each other so that the final result of the calculation is invariably negative. This is to share with theodicism the assumption that there is an implicit scale on which we can place sufferings and the goods they might yield (or for which they may be necessary though unintended by-products).[23]

In the terms of the optimism versus pessimism versus meliorism discussion, we may say that antinatalism is a form of extreme pessimism, while theodicies typically embrace some form of illusory optimism, vigorously criticized already by the early modern thinkers van der Lugt (2021, 2025) places in the tradition of (hopeful) pessimism. However, as pragmatists like James would undoubtedly have suggested had they used the term "antitheodicy," it should be possible to develop a meliorist rather than pessimist version of antitheodicy and antitheodicism.

A radical antitheodicist might, however, challenge this, insisting that even a meliorist harbors illusory beliefs in potential meaning and value that amount to wishful thinking rather than a genuine commitment to taking the reality of suffering seriously. The question then is whether there is a stable middle ground (meliorism) between optimism and pessimism at all. If there is no such middle ground, then antitheodicism runs the risk of either sliding back to theodicism (insofar as it affirms that life might be made valuable and meaningful, after all, and that all existence is not devoid of value because of the inevitability of suffering) or collapsing to the kind of extreme pessimism exemplified by antinatalism (insofar it really does take seriously the full reality of suffering). Antitheodicism might also end up oscillating

---

[22] In her new book on hopeful pessimism, van der Lugt (2025, 9) also notes that the early modern optimism versus pessimism debates receive continuation in the contemporary secular debates on the morality of procreation.

[23] For my transcendental argument against antinatalism as "unthinkable" due to its radical rejection of some of the necessary conditions for the possibility of engaging in serious ethical discussion at all, see Pihlström 2011 and 2025.

between those extremes. I do not think this is necessarily the case, however, and I believe every philosophical effort should be made to articulate, as best we can, the meliorist yet antitheodicist middle path between the implausible and pernicious extremes of optimism/theodicy and pessimism/antinatalism. Nevertheless, within the scope of this introduction, I cannot provide any comprehensive argument that would guarantee success here. Therefore, again, antitheodicism should be regarded as an open research program. It is essential for the antitheodicist to affirm their faith in the possibility of maintaining some form of moral and existential hope even amid the greatest of sufferings, without claiming that such hope ever justifies the suffering. I do concede that this remains a programmatic formulation – definitely not a fully worked-out theory.

What I think is clearer is that the prospects of meliorist antitheodicism depend on the plausibility of a broadly pragmatist approach to the theodicism versus antitheodicism issue. While van der Lugt (2021, 2025), as noted earlier, draws an important distinction between the future-oriented and value-oriented versions of both optimism and pessimism,[24] it is unclear whether this distinction is similarly available for meliorism – or even whether it can be maintained within a pragmatist inquiry into the value (or lack thereof) of life and the world at all, because for pragmatists viewing everything in terms of its conceivable future outcome, this distinction can function only within certain limits. Meliorism, at any rate, needs to be future-oriented, because its key point is that things can and should be made or turned better, even if they will remain far from optimal and the seriousness of evil and suffering must be honestly acknowledged.[25]

5.7. Transcendental Antitheodicism: The "Unthinkability" of Theodicies

The ethical seriousness manifested in antitheodicism, epitomized in the Kantian-Joban virtues of sincerity and honesty, can be summarized as a constant critical focus on the very conditions for the possibility of occupying an ethical stance. In contrast to assuming that suffering – generally or in particular cases – must or ought to make sense, or can be made to make sense by

---

24 In terms of this distinction, the ordinary usage of these terms is future-oriented: optimists are those who believe that things will (inevitably, or at least likely) go well, while pessimists deny this.
25 Meliorism could easily be recommended to the van der Lugtian hopeful pessimist who is – for good reasons – critical of the oft-claimed "duty" to embrace optimism (see van der Lugt 2025, 11–14).

means of a "will to meaning" or by employing our capacities of "meaning-making," and thereby expecting a theodicy (religious or secular) to be delivered, or expecting that if it is not delivered, then the background metaphysics motivating the expectation of delivery (e.g., theism) is defective ("the argument from evil"), we ought to approach suffering by not making such expectations or assumptions at all, recognizing the possibility that suffering *may* be meaningless, even if it may also be meaningful or at least part of a life that as a whole can still be experienced as meaningful. This is to acknowledge the victim and their distinctive perspective on their suffering, including whatever meaning-making capacities they may have and the limits of those capacities. Antitheodicy keeps the framework of such acknowledgment open in the sense of not fixing dogmatically in advance that suffering necessarily is, or is not, meaningful.

A key notion needed here is what we may call *critical distance* (cf. Pihlström and Kivistö 2023). It is the assumption that suffering either is or is not meaningful that needs critique; neither pole of this divide can be taken for granted. This critique itself requires a proper distance: we should not view suffering from too far away, nor by going too close, illusorily assuming that we could simply empathize with others' unique experiences. In brief, we ought to realize that we cannot simply share others' suffering: it is extremely naïve to assume that one could directly partake in another's afflictions no matter how much one cares for them. In this sense, antitheodicism remains – we might say – agnostic about there being meaning in suffering, or at least avoids taking any prior stance on this. Therefore, antitheodicism is necessarily an indirect meta-level position regarding the possible meaning in/of suffering, or lack thereof, insisting that, for ethical reasons, we should not approach suffering (generally or in particular cases) by assuming that it either is or is not meaningful; we should, rather, acknowledge the victim by acknowledging that their suffering may be absurd or meaningless, but we should not claim that it is, or that it isn't.

It is this general way of thinking about the relation between antitheodicism and the meaning of the ethical in our lives that I have tried to capture by speaking of *transcendental antitheodicism*. Given this usage, my approach is "Kantian" though not directly based on Kant's own views (see Chapter 3). It is extremely important to understand correctly what "transcendental" signifies here. In particular, it must not be conflated with "transcendent." Theodicies – and their atheist rejections – reach out toward the transcendent, trying to say something about God (or God's absence, in the case of atheism) and his actual or potential (or missing) reasons for allowing suffering. Antitheodicies, as we have seen, will have none of this. Far from trying to theorize about the transcendent, they examine the issue at a human ethical level, and even more importantly at a Kant-inspired transcendental level, investigating the necessary conditions for the possibility of ethically engaging with suffering in the first place and identifying a critical openness to the possibility of meaninglessness in suffering as one central condition of that kind.

It is, therefore, somewhat misleading to say, as Oliver Wiertz (2021b, 67) does, that transcendental antitheodicism is "the most radical" version of moral antitheodicy. It may be radical in the sense of going to the "roots" (Lat. *radix*) of the problems in theodicies, but this does not mean that transcendental antitheodicism, despite its ethical criticism of theodicies, would, for instance, claim theodicies to be simply immoral, or evil in some extreme sense.[26] Theodicists may very well be morally admirable individuals. They may pursue ethically valuable goals of making a world with evil and suffering more comprehensible to individuals undergoing, or witnessing, experiences of suffering. Yet, according to transcendental antitheodicism, their theodicism is based on a deep-seated illusion in our thinking, the aspiration to climb out of our human standpoint. This is a self-deceptive mischaracterization of our ethical condition and therefore, perhaps, radically mistaken, or even "evil" in the sense of misrepresenting our nature as autonomous moral subjects responsible for the discourses on suffering we engage in. I prefer to say that there is a sense in which this reflection should make theodicies "unthinkable" as serious ethical options. This is very different from saying that theodicies are just false or morally wrong. The unthinkability at issue operates at a transcendental level, pertaining to the constitutive conditions of our ability to pursue the kinds of moral values that even theodicists may be committed to pursuing.

The antitheodicist should, then, firmly agree with Samuel Shearn (2013, 439, 451) that antitheodicies offer no "moral high ground." There is no self-satisfied position open to us if we are seriously engaged in an antitheodicist exploration of evil and suffering. Shearn plausibly notes that if theodicists are "comfortably detached academics" contemplating suffering they themselves need not endure, so are, of course, antitheodicists who have "the leisure to write at length about the immorality of theodicy" (ibid., 451). The gaze of moral critique should, and can, exclude no one. Even Shearn, however, shares some of the problems identified in Franklin's (2020) discussion earlier, because he construes Dostoevsky's Ivan Karamazov as criticizing the morality of God's creating the world at all insofar as there is going to be innocent suffering in the creation, such as a child's tears (Shearn 2013, 453–454). This "handing back" of the ticket should, however, be focused on the morality

---

26 Compare this to the Kantian notion of "radical evil."

of our human ways of construing the possible meaningfulness of suffering and *our* acceptance of a scheme of redemption ultimately guaranteeing such meaningfulness.[27] Ivan's view, on my reading, is not a statement about how God (if God exists) should answer the question of whether to create a world at all, but a serious examination, by a morally concerned and simultaneously a deeply flawed and confused individual, of how we human beings ought to regard the suffering of others we see around us, and how we ought to consider our ethical and religious (and secular) ways of conceptualizing our lives in a world in which such suffering is real.

This brings us to Nick Trakakis's penetrating analysis of Ivan Karamazov's antitheodicy.[28] Discussing Dostoevsky's character, who in *The Brothers Karamazov* "hands back his ticket," refusing to accept God's harmony and salvation if their price is the suffering of a single innocent child, Trakakis refers to Zachary Braiterman's (1998) view according to which (on Trakakis's reading) "the project of theodicy is rejected outright – the project, that is, of identifying God's (possible or actual) reasons for permitting evil" (Trakakis 2021, 700). Saying that theodicy is "rejected outright" is to say that it is not, and cannot be, seriously considered at all as a possible view to adopt, as long as we are trying to engage with suffering ethically. Nor can the skeptical theist suggestion that there may be God's hidden reasons somewhere there beyond our grasp be taken any more seriously than theodicies proper. The problem lies in "something much deeper" than the mere "hubris of claiming to understand the ways of God," something related to our understanding of the very concepts of "God" and "evil" (ibid.). The well-known reference to Dostoevsky illustrates the key idea that it is "illegitimate or unintelligible" to even employ the idea of "God permitting evil for the sake of a greater good" (ibid., 701). This idea is not merely intellectually mistaken, and not even to be rejected on first-order moral grounds, as we would reject, for instance, some

---

27 I am not claiming anything about how Dostoevsky should be interpreted but again only loosely referring to this famous example of antitheodicism. See Chapter 3 on Ivan Karamazov.

28 Trakakis is without question one of the leading scholars writing on antitheodicy today. The only reason why I have not more extensively dwelled on his treatment of antitheodicy (e.g., Trakakis 2013, 2017, 2018) in this book is that I more or less agree with him about almost everything. (For his recent reflection on the critical dialogue between theodicist "idealism" and antitheodicist "existentialism," see Trakakis 2023.) However, my own transcendental approach, and especially my combination of pragmatist and transcendental methods of argumentation, is somewhat different from his project.

"normal" moral illegitimacy. Something is much more profoundly – monstrously – wrong in the theodicist approach employing such an idea.

While Trakakis does not use the term "unthinkable," we may say that for Dostoevsky's Ivan, it is unthinkable to accept that the suffering of an innocent child could be justified or forgiven – even if such divine justice were to be manifested right before his eyes (ibid., 705). Ivan's simply not accepting this ought to be seen as more fundamental than, say, any theological conception of the divinity; the "handing back" of the ticket draws a boundary of decency between what may be considered and what must be ruled out in advance as a monstrosity not to be considered. Theodicies, in short, are not false but monstrous. Reflecting on theodicy versus antitheodicy therefore brings us to the ultimate limit of ethical discussion. It is important to note, once again, that this is not at all to join the atheist theodicy-driven argumentation according to which we should reject theism because of the argument from evil. While Ivan has often been regarded as a "protest atheist," Trakakis calls Ivan's position a "radicalized" antitheodicy; in my view it comes close to transcendental antitheodicism according to which theodicies are unthinkable or impossible rather than simply false or wrong.

Ivan, as Trakakis notes, does not reject God's existence when he "absolutely renounces" any higher harmony (ibid., 708). Assuming that Christianity entails the kind of harmony rejected by Ivan, this does entail rejecting Christianity – even if it is true (ibid., 709) – though we must again remember that there are interpretations of Christianity (and other religions, including, of course, Judaism) that are antitheodicist rather than theodicist. However, more significantly, whether or not Christianity postulating such a harmony (or any theodicist account claiming that evil and suffering will finally be overcome and/or that we can be eventually reconciled with them) is true ultimately plays no role in determining whether or not we ought to accept it.[29] Failing to refuse to accept the theodicist harmony – failing to return the ticket – "would be a betrayal of the sufferers" (ibid., 710), and this is the sense in which theodicies engage in speculations that (in Phillips's memorable words) ought not even to be contemplated. The issue thus goes deeper than questions about truth and falsity.

---

29 Interestingly, Trakakis (2021, 711) compares Ivan's rejection of Christianity even if it were true to Dostoevsky's own view expressed in a letter in 1854: "*Even if someone were to prove to me that the truth lay outside Christ, I should prefer to remain with Christ than with the truth*" (italics by Trakakis). The concept of truth, of course, would need further reflection here (e.g., in terms of pragmatism: cf. Pihlström 2021).

We may, however, ask how and whence Trakakis, or Ivan, gets the normative force for the claim that theodicist harmony *ought to* be rejected. It might be better to say that Ivan simply does not accept such harmony (either in its Christian or other forms), refusing any reconciliation of the child's tears. Engaging in *any* serious ethical discussion can, then, be taken to presuppose that such harmony *is* rejected to begin with – that is, ruled out as unthinkable. This formulation, again, is one step removed from a straightforward moral condemnation of theodicies as wrong (or even as "obscene" or immoral), because our very ability to engage in any moral discussion whatsoever is at stake here. Trakakis joins Dostoevsky in maintaining that moral seriousness presupposes that we abandon theodicies: "For after 'Auschwitz', after the horrors recounted by Ivan and replayed countlessly on history's slaughter-bench, theodicy is not so much insufficient or falsified, but nauseating and obscene, to the point of being beyond belief *even if* true, *especially if* true" (ibid., 720; original emphases). Even if theodicies were true (whatever that could mean), they would have to be rejected. If my suggestions are on the right track, such rejection can rationally only take place at a transcendental level, concerning the conditions that make truth-seeking and moral pursuits themselves possible for us.

Obviously, Trakakis's antitheodicist analysis (with which I am largely in agreement) by no means exhausts the immense richness of Dostoevsky's engagement with the problem of suffering in *The Brothers Karamazov*. For example, Elena Namli defends a somewhat different approach to the issue by arguing, possibly slightly surprisingly, that regarding Dostoevsky's antitheodicy, it is Alexei Karamazov, rather than Ivan, that should be considered the key character in the novel. According to Namli, it is in Alexei in particular that the famous Dostoevskyan theme that everyone is guilty before all and for all (cf. also Pihlström 2011) finds its central expression, and his rejection of the immorality of theodicies that Ivan (rightly) emphasizes is the radical personal responsibility for everyone that we associate with the kind of ethics we later find in Levinas (see Namli 2022, especially 28; cf. again Chapter 3).[30] Though Namli does not put the matter exactly in these terms, I would suggest that it is the assumption – prevalent both in ordinary morality and in academic ethics – that there is some reasonable "measure" to what is "enough" for us in bearing moral responsibility that is rejected here. Antitheodicism, by reminding us of the immeasurability of suffering and the disproportionality

---

30 Another interesting suggestion by Namli (2022) is the critical comparison by Dostoevsky and Tolstoy from the perspective of a distinction between individual (and politically naïve) and social or structural suffering.

of any alleged harmony and the kind of innocent suffering Ivan appeals to, also urges us that our moral responsibility is infinite, or at least as indefinitely deep as suffering itself. There is no limit to what is sufficient, no measure of any kind – neither for suffering nor for the ethical response required from us by the face of the other. In morality, we can never say that we have done what we ought to have done, that is, that we have done enough. Dostoevsky's idea that my guilt for everyone else is always the greatest is a solemn literary expression of this view. While it may never be practically applicable in real life, it may be suggested that something in the seriousness of the ethical is lost if we fail to appreciate this idea.

We have seen how transcendental antitheodicism, claiming theodicism to be unthinkable rather than just wrong, operates at a meta-level in comparison to all "first-order" moral criticisms of the "offensiveness" of theodicies. Antitheodicism, though emerging from ethical concern, must not be moralizing, even though it should, and does, remind us of our absolute responsibility. We have to be careful, however, when articulating the relationship between moral and transcendental antitheodicisms. While the former claims theodicies to be morally problematic or even evil, the latter indirectly suggests that theodicism, by failing to recognize the (potential) meaninglessness of suffering, violates the necessary conditions for the possibility of our so much as adopting an ethical stance to the world. However, even this distinction cannot be easily maintained, because we are always already operating "within the ethical" even when presenting meta-level transcendental criticism against positions that we take to be morally illegitimate (albeit in a sense impossible) transgressions of the limits of the ethical. There is no escaping of the ethical stance the antitheodicist claims the theodicist tries (in vain) to escape. Accordingly, the distinction between moral and transcendental antitheodicisms is not a clean dualism between two different levels of discourse but largely a matter of emphasis. Even the transcendental antitheodicist should be able to view themselves as operating, always already, within a normative sphere of moral critique. (This, indeed, is part of the reason why it is transcendental: the claim is, ultimately, that morality is ubiquitous, transcendentally – constitutively – present in everything human.) It is, then, a moral requirement for us to view our ethical condition along the lines of transcendental antitheodicism, even though we should not, when adopting such a view, make any easy or direct moralizing claims about others' failures. It is morally vital for us to get the "meaning of the ethical" right at a transcendental level.[31]

---

31 I am here indebted to Pöykkö's (2023) transcendental reading of Levinas and conversations with him on Levinas and antitheodicy.

Therefore, the moral horror we may find the only appropriate reaction to some of the obscenest pronouncements of theodicists is ultimately entangled with the transcendental account, though we should, nevertheless, avoid simple moralizing as much as we can.

Accordingly, when joining Levinas in insisting that a theodicist justification of others' suffering is the source of all immorality, we should not interpret the concept of "source" at work here in any causal or factual sense but as an articulation of the transcendental sense in which the very idea of the ethical depends on an antitheodicist recognition of the reality of suffering. Theodicism makes itself a (or, better, the) source of all immorality by depriving us of our human capacity of viewing the world, especially suffering, ethically at all. Yet, our need to maintain such capacities of viewing our world morally is itself a moral need. Even the most abstractly formulated transcendental criticism of theodicism is at the same time a moral critique of our lives. We should not flatten the discourse on suffering by reductively confusing the levels of discourse of first-order moral evaluation and second-order transcendental conditions for the possibility of such evaluation, but we should acknowledge that when engaging in the latter we are inevitably also engaging in the former and that these levels are in the last analysis inseparably intertwined. At the same time, we should constantly keep in mind that even the theodicist's moral motivations may be admirable and that our transcendental critique should never turn moralizing.

It remains an open question – to be revisited again and again – how far and in what sense exactly the transcendental criticism of theodicies based on their failure to account for the necessary conditions for the possibility of an ethical stance is itself a moral criticism, too. When engaging in theodicies we engage in speculations that "we should not even contemplate" (Phillips 1977), or, in Gaita's (2004 [1991]) terms (which he does not apply to the theodicy context, though), in thinking "unthinkable" thoughts we should fear to think, lest we become people we should fear to become. Similarly, as we have seen, Levi (1988 [1986]) regarded as "monstrous" the idea that he would have survived the Holocaust – teleologically, due to providence – in order to be able to bear witness; attributing such providentiality to the flow of absurd and violent historical events would be tantamount to endorsing the pseudo-religious and superstitious worldview epitomized in prisoner Kuhn's prayer. In order to maintain decency in sharing a world with other vulnerable human beings – in sharing "our common humanity" (Gaita 2000) – we should recognize their (our) possibly ending up as victims of entirely unmerited suffering, and harboring theodicies violates this basic acknowledgment of others' perspectives on the world. It matters to us enormously, ethically, whether we view our relation to the world in terms of an antitheodicist or a theodicist outlook, even though the distinction between those two is primarily a meta-level transcendental issue, rather than a merely first-order moral (let alone moralizing) one. Moreover, in engaging in the kind of antitheodicist ethical and transcendental critique I have outlined here, we are at the same time seeking to ameliorate our ethical condition, to see the world we live in more lucidly and more responsibly. This is a thoroughly ethical challenge, not to be safely accounted for in terms of any purely metaethical inquiry from above.

What exactly does it, or could it, mean to claim theodicies to be "unthinkable," then? Are they comparable to other cases of morally horrendous views, such as Holocaust denialism or the idea (invoking a well-known thought experiment in moral philosophy) that it might be permissible to kill an innocent person in order to save the lives of five others needing organ transplantations by taking her/his organs?[32] Certainly, as already acknowledged above, it is not obviously indecent to be a theodicist, as many morally admirable individuals do subscribe to (religious or secular) theodicies of some kind, and many of them continue to engage in sophisticated philosophical and theological reflection on them. However, antitheodicism entertains the (distant) *hope* for a cultural change involving a deep conceptual shift that would eventually bring us from viewing the rejection of theodicies as unthinkable (as in premodern or early modern societies and their philosophico-theological discourses) to viewing the acceptance of theodicies as unthinkable, precisely due to their tendency to overlook others' suffering in its shocking reality and meaninglessness.

In addition to this vague hope, we might say that antitheodicism takes seriously the *fear* of becoming theodicist, as well as the fear (encountered above) of theodicies always returning. Following Gaita's (2004 [1991], Chapter 17) view that there are thoughts we should, or can only, fear to think, we might express the ethical "unthinkability" of theodicism by saying that if we merely entertained (however hypothetically) the thought that (say) the Holocaust *might* be morally justified in terms of some "greater good," or that it *might*, just might, have been an appropriate price to pay for some overall cosmic or historical benefit, we would already have lost touch with moral reality. If I failed to find it unthinkable to begin with to postulate some possible moral justification for the Holocaust along these lines, I would be entirely lost, knowing nothing not only about the Holocaust itself but about the world I live in. What is at issue

---

32 The latter kind of thought experiments, presupposing something like "Singerian" consequentialism, are heavily criticized as "unthinkable thoughts" rendering the practices of academic moral philosophy corrupt by Gaita (2004 [1991], chapter 17). See Pihlström 2025 for further reflection.

here is the sense in which our moral seriousness is constituted by our fearing to become a person who would have lost their touch with moral reality. Entertaining the mere thought that the Holocaust might have a moral justification would be a thought that I ought to fear. Becoming a theodicist thinking such thoughts would also be something that I should fear, rather than merely block by means of an intellectual argument.

This also shows that there are limits to how far we can really *argue* for antitheodicism. We must arguably already occupy a moral standpoint in order to be able to engage in any ethical argument, and insofar as antitheodicism is a transcendental condition for the possibility of the former, it cannot be directly supported by the latter. This seems to be the outcome of the discussion in this section. One option here is to view antitheodicism and the ethical stance itself as *co-constitutive*: neither can be regarded as fundamental or primary in relation to the other. Methodologically, to make sense of this, we are well advised to construe the transcendental method itself in a pragmatic and thus antifoundationalist manner, giving up any foundationalist pursuit of apodictic certainty. We can only gradually and fallibly engage in the neverending process of seeking to understand and ameliorate our moral condition from within it.

This methodological stance, an integration of pragmatist and transcendental argumentation, is also necessary for us to be able to maintain that there is a sense in which theodicism may be claimed to be "unthinkable" and that, simultaneously, the concept of unthinkability – or the distinction between the thinkable and the unthinkable – must already be available to us within a sphere of moral reflection that itself depends on our having adopted antitheodicism. Without antitheodicism, we cannot claim theodicies to be unthinkable, but without doing this, we cannot embrace antitheodicism. Accordingly, these moves have to be made in tandem, and this provides, in my view, an indirect argument for synthesizing pragmatist and transcendental approaches to the problem of suffering.

This discussion arrives, I think – via a rather different route – at an agreement with Gabriel Echazú's (2024a) view according to which at least some attempts to claim antitheodicy to be question-begging fail. Instead of being simply vulnerable to the kind of question-beggingness claims exemplified by critics like Mark Simpson (2009), a kind of circularity (albeit self-strengthening rather than vicious) can be said to be inherent in transcendental antitheodicism finding theodicies unthinkable to begin with. Echazú shows how such criticism overlooks the key point in antitheodicies as criticizing the entire theodicy framework instead of presenting (like atheist critics of theistic theodicies) arguments within that framework. Exactly as I have done in this book (and earlier), Echazú (2024a, 1-8) recognizes that atheists attacking theodicies engage "in theodical discourse practice" as much as theists defending theodicies do. While he does not present antitheodicies or antitheodicism as transcendental, he appropriately notes the "meta-level" character of antitheodicy: what is at issue is the legitimacy of the theodicy project itself, not any particular argument presupposing that "game."

In a sense, antitheodicism is, then, *metaphilosophical* by nature. The project of antitheodicism, transcendentally developed, entails that in a certain sense antitheodicies *must* beg the question against theodicies, because there can be no firmer ground to base those arguments on than something that antitheodicies insist on, that is, the recognition of others' suffering in its immeasurability and possible meaninglessness.[33]

However, it is at this point that we should, once again, also avoid any temptation to claim to occupy a morally higher ground. Finding ethics a realm of absolute infinite duty (in a Levinasian sense) instead of a matter of relational, conditional, and measurable (commensurate) "trade-offs" between costs and benefits,[34] we should not only reject the notion of "price" implicitly assumed in theodicism but also lucidly realize that "every man has his price" – that is, an ethical breaking point after which they will be ready to sacrifice their most central moral values to considerations of utility or personal benefit.[35] It is part of our ethical task of self-understanding to acknowledge that we inevitably fall short of the requirements of ethics – that is, that we do have our price, no matter how strongly we are against the idea of portraying ethics in terms of any such price. In other words, while we might take ethics to be ubiquitous or all-encompassing, we also know that in our lives it has its limits. We are capable of doing the unthinkable, and as Levi's Holocaust writings show us, even the strongest can be broken. Shockingly, as Orwell's character Winston in *Nineteen Eighty-Four* (1949) arrives at his breaking point in torture,

---

33 Echazú does not put the matter in these terms, also because he does not explicitly thematize transcendental antitheodicism. Analogously, Kant's transcendental idealism – and his entire critical system – in a sense beg the question against radical skepticism, because no proof of the reality of the external world is provided. What is provided by Kant is not a refutation of external world skepticism but a complex argument responding to the question *how* (not *whether*) it is possible for us to have cognitive experience of external objects.

34 In addition to Levinas, we may here refer to Wittgenstein's 1929 "A Lecture on Ethics" (in Wittgenstein 1993), crucially distinguishing between absolute and relative value judgments and finding only the former a matter of ethics.

35 Kant (1793-94, 6:39) refers to "[a] member of the English Parliament" as someone to whom this phrase is attributed: "Every man has his price, for which he sells himself." In the editors' notes (ibid., 86n19), it is explained that the person Kant cites is Sir Robert Walpole.

he can only say, "Do it to Julia!", being ready to sacrifice what is dearest and most deeply valuable to him. There is, then, some point, for any of us, after which everything is for sale. Only an antitheodicist meliorist approach can, I believe, both admit our human finitude at this fundamental level and remain committed to a never-ending struggle for moral amelioration.

These reflections also bring us back to the "return" of theodicy (discussed earlier in this chapter). Antitheodicism emphasizes the pricelessness and incommensurability of suffering there is no price that could justify suffering in its Levinasian "uselessness." Therefore, if everyone has their price, theodicist logic reigns. If anyone can be broken, no absolute value remains – no level of the ethical that would be independent of the trade-offs and prices of this world of power relations and always (at best) partial moral commitments and compromises. At this point, our investigation of antitheodicism is entangled with the radical evil in the "human heart" that Kant analyzed in his *Religionsschrift*, and the idea of our inescapable "transcendental guilt," a guilt inherent in our merely being human, not based on anything particular that we did or failed to do (Pihlström 2011). These are also ideas that antitheodicism should continue to reflect on.

5.8. Meaning

When saying that antitheodicism questions the theodicist assumption that there always is, at least potentially, meaning in suffering – or, more generally, that we should be able to view the world in which suffering exists as meaningful despite the horrors – as well as the atheist use of this assumption as a premise in an argument challenging theism for its failure to deliver the meaningfulness it promises, I am *not* saying that antitheodicism would simply claim that we live in an absurd, meaningless world. On the contrary, our living, inescapably, in a world of human meanings needs constant *critique*. A naïve faith in our meaning-making capacities even amid the most absurd and cruel circumstances is theodicist to the core. While it is always a delicate matter to criticize Holocaust literature, especially survivors' writings, it seems to me (and I am hardly alone here) that such a theodicist faith was expressed by Viktor Frankl (1969) in his views on the "will to meaning" based on his survivor experience. The concept of "meaning-making" has indeed been associated with Frankl's *Man's Search for Meaning* (1946).

In contrast, the picture of meaning we get from another Holocaust survivor's, Levi's, above-cited work is strikingly different. We may read both *If This Is a Man* (Levi 1996 [1958]) and later reflections such as *The Drowned and the Saved* (Levi 1988 [1986]), discussed earlier in this chapter, as an extended argument suggesting that the evil and suffering that took place in the

Holocaust exceed our human boundaries of meaningfulness and meaning-making, destroying the moral and conceptual capacities we need for making sense of the world. An experience of a colossal injustice at a fundamental metaphysical level – not just in society but in the world in general – may shatter our ability to comprehend the world, not only our meaning-making itself but the possibility of distinguishing between meaningfulness and meaninglessness. The entire scale of meaning on which we place the events of our lives may be fragmented.[36] A critical distance to this entire scale is crucial here: we should not be simply immersed in meanings in life that we just assume to be there, but we should not view the meaningfulness versus meaninglessness of our lives (and the world) from an absolutely detached perspective, either, because then we lose the possibility of making distinctions between meanings and their absences. If we adopt a sufficiently far-away vantage point (a God's-Eye View), then there will be no human meanings of any kind left.

There is, then, an enormous gulf separating the disturbingly "self-help"-like insistence on the possibility of meaning-making in suffering – even the most horrible suffering – that we find in Frankl, on the one hand, and Levi's steadfast refusal (not far from Job's sincerity) to attach any meaning to his or his fellows' sufferings, especially his survival, which he found simply a result of random chance and good luck in absurd circumstances, maintaining, as we saw, that any teleological attribution of providence to his surviving would be "monstrous." However, even the Levian antitheodicist does not categorically deny meaning. There is no way of escaping the fact that as humans we live in a world of meanings and that we "make meaning" all the time. What we do need is a critical antitheodicist stance – at a critical distance – to that meaning-making itself, a recognition that no processes of meaning-making, no matter how natural and inescapable they are for us, are innocent. What is humanly natural is precisely what needs critique. And precisely by rendering suffering and historical evils elements of an allegedly harmonious world in which things make sense, ultimately if not immediately or apparently, we run the risk of unethically failing to acknowledge others' unique perspectives on the world. This happens particularly easily when we attribute a theodicist justification to others' sufferings.

Finally, the theodicist might suggest that even the pointlessness or meaninglessness of suffering could itself be part of the ultimate account of reality (available from a God's-Eye View) and thus rendered an element of a world in which everything eventually falls into its place in a harmonious totality.

---

36 On the problem of evil as a problem of finding the world intelligible or comprehensible (or finding life meaningful) at all, see again, e.g., Neiman 2002; Cottingham 2017; Snellman 2023.

However, if this were the case, then the pointlessness at issue would be merely apparent. For example, the fact that there could be meaningless evil and suffering (resulting from the misuse of our freedom, for instance) would then ultimately serve the theodicy-driven point that it is better (and thus "more meaningful") to have a world with human beings equipped with free will and responsibility than a world with no such freedom. This would then be viewed as the supreme value that God has chosen to consider more important than preventing horrendous suffering. The antitheodicist would hardly be convinced by this line of argument, because it would practically amount to disregarding the genuine meaninglessness of suffering and to putting evil into some kind of positive "use," after all. A mere verbal trick cannot save the theodicist from this argument, but conversely the antitheodicist should also acknowledge the limits of philosophical argumentation: the theodicist could always simply reinterpret the antitheodicist's appeals to the meaninglessness of suffering as mere manifestations of our finite human capacities, that is, our inability to view things from a transcendent divine perspective.

We should, therefore, cherish no illusions about being able to conclusively demonstrate that theodicism is wrong. Indeed, if theodicism is, as I have argued, unthinkable in the sense of lying outside the sphere of meaningful ethical argumentation, violating the constitutive conditions of sound and ethically decent argumentation, there is no way in which it could possibly be argumentatively shown to be mistaken, because any argument depends on our already having rejected theodicism. (On the other hand, the availability of *this* meta-level consideration might eventually count as an argument against theodicism – and in any case we should recall the point made earlier about the antitheodicist's transcendental and the moral projects being entangled with each other.) In any event, we should, instead of cherishing naïve expectations of conclusive refutation of theodicism, develop and maintain a critical attitude to our uses of the concept of meaning and our practices of meaning-making and constantly seek alternatives to our habitual ways of viewing others' sufferings in terms of our own schemes of meaningfulness, being painfully conscious of our unavoidable tendency to try to render these sufferings meaningful and of the (related) tendency of theodicies to return as soon as we rest satisfied with having left them behind.

We might also say that in the end the only way to "argue" for antitheodicism – given that the pragmatist and transcendental argumentation strategy pursued in this book is inevitably limited[37] – is to develop ways of remaining

---

37 On the limits of argumentation as a metaphilosophical phenomenon, see Pihlström 2025, especially Chapter 4.

open to viewing the world without postulating theodicist meanings, instead of just claiming theodicies to be false or wrong. In Arvi Särkelä's (2025) intriguing terms, we could then see antitheodicism as a "critical gesture" comparable to what Särkelä describes as Wittgenstein's gesture in suggesting that what is usually seen as progress could also be seen as catastrophic.[38] The "same world" – that is, the same empirical facts, including suffering, especially in history, could (in Wittgensteinian terms) be *seen as* either divinely permitted or justifiable and thus meaningful or as unjustifiable and meaningless. It would be a misunderstanding to expect a conclusive argument; what remains possible is a new way of seeing (available through a critical gesture) that changes everything.[39] The theodicy "aspect" and the antitheodicy "aspect" of the world would then be equally possible as ways of seeing the world "as" what it is, comparable to Wittgenstein's (1953, Part II, xi) duck-rabbit picture (employed by Särkelä in his analysis). Similarly, optimism and pessimism could be understood as "aspects" under which the world could also be seen as either valuable or lacking in value. Then, meliorism, as the critical middle path favored in this book, would be a critical gesture avoiding both – the only difference being that in the case of theodicism and antitheodicism, there is no obvious middle ground available (though, recall, the antitheodicist need not and should not simply claim the world to be meaningless but should rather maintain a critical stance to our unavoidable meaning-making practices). In a sense, meliorism allows for a "*Gestaltswitch*" between optimism and pessimism – these aspects "lighting up" – and in principle antitheodicism allows this, too, by not categorically denying meaning.

This critical stance might even enable us to appreciate the point – emphasized by Gaita (2004 [1991]), among others, based on his reading of Levi – that goodness itself, just as suffering, is "pointless," and in that sense meaningless.[40] We do not aim at being good in order to use that aim, or whatever might be achieved by successfully pursuing it, for some other, presumably

---

38 Särkelä's point of departure is Wittgenstein's (1998, 64) remark on "[t]he truly apocalyptic view."

39 Would theodicy then, instead of being unthinkable (as suggested above and in Pihlström 2025), be something like an instance of what Wittgenstein calls "aspect-blindness"? Finding it unthinkable could, on the other hand, be understood as equivalent to maintaining that the world should not be "seen as" theodicistically justifiable, that is, that one ought not to let the theodicy "aspect" "lighten up" in one's world-viewing.

40 One relevant, though indirect, background idea here is Iris Murdoch's (2007 [1971]) account of the "sovereignty" of the good. "The humble man," "the kind of man who is most likely of all to become good," Murdoch concludes, "sees the pointlessness of virtue and its unique value and the endless extent of its demand" (ibid., 101).

more important purpose; in this sense, being good is not and can never be "meaningful." This is, indirectly, one of the deepest insights derivable from antitheodicism. Taking others' suffering seriously is to acknowledge that doing whatever lies within our power to, melioristically, alleviate that suffering cannot serve any other purpose or have any other "meaning" than itself.

The concept of meaning, as used in this section and throughout this chapter, is of course elusive. Sometimes we use "meaning" to simply denote semantic meaning, sometimes the kind of teleological structures of significance that our "meaning-making" processes also exhibit. Even when rejecting the kind of pursuit of meaning(fulness) exemplified by theodicism, we need the concept of meaning to account for the suffering whose possible meaninglessness we should recognize. Sometimes the fact that a given act or event can (decently, appropriately) only be described as evil – because any milder description, such as a reference to the violation of human rights – would fail to do justice to the victims, is an ineliminable part of the "meaning" of that act or event.[41] Obviously, we must conceptualize even the most insane incidents of evil as "meaningful" in this sense. Moreover, there can be unbearable suffering going beyond all our boundaries of meaning-making that is unbearable precisely because it has the kind of "meaning" it does (see Williams 2006); its meaning as some special kind of evil could be constitutive of its unbearability, and even of its rendering its victim's world or life incomprehensible at an existential level.

Antitheodicism, then, is a never-ending critical reflection on the various, possibly conflicting, kinds of meaning that we, contingently or inevitably, attach to the events of our lives and histories needing our constant ethical attention. It is part of our critical recognition of the transcendentally constitutive status of antitheodicism that we also acknowledge the impossibility of avoiding our reliance on the concept of meaning. For better or worse, we human beings live in a world of meanings.

---

41 I am again indebted to Gaita's (2000, 2004 [1991]) formulations in phrasing this point. According to Gaita, when we speak of the victims of evil such as, for instance, slavery or the Holocaust, we would fail to even properly begin to describe the ways those victims were wronged by saying that their human rights were violated.

Chapter 6
CONCLUSION

After some conceptual preliminaries (Chapter 2) and a historical sketch of the emergence of antitheodicies from Kant to Levinas and the twentieth century (Chapter 3), Chapter 4 emphasized the contemporary relevance of the (anti)theodicy issue by introducing the concepts of secular theodicy and secular theodicism and providing reasons to critically examine our tendencies to impose a theodicist logic on our individual and social actions responding to others' sufferings. Examples of secular theodicism were identified, and some important research questions for pragmatist antitheodicism in particular were formulated. A brief case study on the ethics of war and peace was employed in Chapter 4 to argue that secular theodicism seems to be at work both in just war theory and pacifism. Antitheodicism was then (admittedly tentatively and programmatically) in Chapter 5 claimed to be a pragmatic and transcendental condition for the possibility of ethical sincerity. The fifth chapter also explored fundamental issues pertaining to what we may call the philosophical status of antitheodicism, including the "unthinkability" of theodicism and the unavoidability of meaning and meaning-making to which we must, however, take a critical stance.

Clearly, despite my emphasis on the real-world relevance of antitheodicy, my aim in this book has not been to settle complex ethical issues about, for example, war and peace (or the ethical problems of secular theodicies generally, such as those relating to pandemics or other health-care issues, for that matter) but merely to emphasize the sense in which identifying secular theodicies is directly relevant to these and many other real-world topics. For example, both pacifism and just war theory were tentatively claimed to be grounded in secular theodicism, and further ethical reflection on such questions of life and death should, I have tried to argue, be based on critical pragmatist antitheodicism rather than theodicism. Moreover, this should not even be regarded as a genuine choice, insofar as we are to remain within the bounds of serious moral discourse. Based on a transcendental argument for antitheodicism as constitutive of ethical decency, we should move into a culture that views theodicism as the "dead" (instead of "live") option it is[1] – due to its ethical unthinkability (as reflected on toward the end of Chapter 5).

Ultimately, the choice between theodicism and antitheodicism is a choice regarding the ways in which we may and should see the nature of morality and its place in our lives. Does morality require an extra-moral framework of meaningfulness or intelligibility, or is it autonomous and self-standing, itself the ultimate source of any meaning or intelligibility there may be in our lives? This could be conceptualized as a question concerning how morality should (in Wittgensteinian terms) be "seen as," a question requiring a "critical gesture" (cf. Särkelä 2025), as suggested in the concluding section of Chapter 5.

There are critics of antitheodicy maintaining that we still need an intelligible order of meaningfulness in order to make sense of ethics.[2] I am not convinced that we can consistently both entertain the central idea of theodicist thinking that morality requires such a wider framework of intelligibility and take the antitheodicist ethical charge seriously. As authors like Susan Neiman (2002) and Lauri Snellman (2023) show, and as has been emphasized throughout this work, the critique of theodicies focuses on comprehensibility, that is, on the very idea that we should – or that we are entitled to – presuppose an "intelligible order" of reality. This is the ultimate reason why explicitly Christian attempts at a theodicy (even unorthodox ones), such as Eleonore Stump's (2010) narrative theodicy, fail. Such arguments depend too much on a Christian idea of redemption in order to be relevant to counter the general antitheodicist critique challenging the assumption of intelligibility (or, in other words, challenging the postulation of meaningfulness; cf. again Section 5.8).[3] On the other hand, as we have also seen, the antitheodicist does not have to claim that the world in general is absurd or unintelligible; it is sufficient to maintain that there are, or at least can be, cases of irreconcilably meaningless unmerited suffering (e.g., the Holocaust) that no one can decently claim to be forgiven or redeemed – and thus to join Ivan Karamazov in handing back any "ticket" that depends on the view that everything must in the end be reconciled. This is not to deny that there is also deep value and

---

1 The vocabulary of live and dead options is, of course, adopted from William James's (1979 [1897]) "will to believe" discussion.
2 See, in particular, the recent paper by Aakko (2025), defending a theistic theodicism that nevertheless appreciates the antitheodicist arguments appealing to meaningless suffering. Aakko's key move here is to view the intelligible order as "decentered," best analyzed in aesthetic terms.
3 I find Aakko's (2025) position problematic for similar reasons, despite her apparently sincere willingness to accommodate the antitheodicist insistence on human fragility and incompleteness in her primarily theodicist framework.

meaningfulness in the world – and not even to deny the fact that for some individuals the pursuit of theodicy might be a way of searching such value and meaningfulness, or a desperate quest for meaning amid meaninglessness, which we should appreciate even when remaining critical of it.[4]

Importantly, then, we may easily imagine moral and transcendental antitheodicists challenging the idea that moral agency requires a larger context of an intelligible order. For a Kantian, for instance, morality cannot be based on *anything* external to itself. Therefore, the question we have been preoccupied with throughout this book is ultimately a question about what kind of picture of morality we are committed to. Let me conclude by brief comments on this issue, thus also summarizing some of the main ideas developed in this volume.

Theodicism can be taken to claim, in the final analysis, that morality (especially moral agency, or ethical evaluation generally) presupposes an intelligible order, such as the metaphysical framework provided by Christian theism or some secular proxy. Antitheodicism, in contrast, can be taken to challenge this claim by suggesting that morality presupposes, on the contrary, our recognizing the reality of evil and suffering that can, at least sometimes, be meaningless or absurd, without any intelligibility – or even something that might destroy our faith in any meaningful structures of reality (not only theism but also, say, any teleological conception of history). According to antitheodicism, morality (or ethics) is self-standing and autonomous rather than subordinated to a wider framework of intelligibility. Morality itself is, and can only be, *the* framework within which morality makes sense. If morality did require a wider order of intelligibility in order to be real or meaningful for us, then it would cease to be morality in the absolute sense in which something might be morally required of us no matter what other (non-moral) values it might conflict with. To think otherwise is already to reach beyond morality and thus to what I have called "the unthinkable" (cf. also Pihlström 2025).

This suggestion is also related to the question of the nature of the philosophy of religion, which, after all, is the home for much of the theodicy versus antitheodicy debate, both historically and today. I have repeatedly emphasized that antitheodicies need not be atheistic, and that typical atheist arguments from evil are, indeed, implicitly theodicist in the sense of normatively expecting theism to deliver a theodicy. Conversely, there are not only

---

4 Nor does antitheodicy need to be committed to any particular view regarding the sense, if any, in which evil itself is unintelligible or incomprehensible. See Chignell's (2019b) detailed analysis of this issue in relation to the concepts of the radicality and the banality of evil.

philosophers (relatively) sympathetic to religion or theism (such as Phillips) but also theologians (e.g., Surin 1986) who have vigorously criticized theodicies (see also Koistinen 2022). The antitheodicy discussion is thus one of the contexts within which the relation between theology and philosophy (of religion) can be further pursued.

I have also argued that the theodicism versus antitheodicism opposition is ethically more fundamental than the theism versus atheism one. However, to subscribe to this meta-level view is to admit that in some sense the philosophy of religion must be fully secular and thus cannot be entirely neutral with regard to the basic controversies in the field. From a non-secular perspective, such as "Christian philosophy," according to which Christian philosophers can argue from Christian premises (see, e.g., Plantinga 2000), it can hardly be said that any other issue could be more fundamental than the one between theism and atheism. Does this entail that we must first settle the issue between secular and non-secular approaches, after all, and only then move on to consider (anti)theodicy? I do not think so, but of course I can reasonably maintain *this* view only within a broadly conceived secularism, which, however, is not the militant atheist secularism its opponents might like to see it as. We may say that antitheodicism and the kind of meta-level non-militant, humanist secularism it seems to presuppose are mutually (reciprocally) contained in each other. Antitheodicism may not be religiously or theologically entirely neutral, as it must remain humanistic (as explained in Chapter 5), but it certainly need not be anti-religious. It cannot place any divinely established harmonious order of the world prior to the human need to respond ethically to others' suffering independently of any metaphysical commitment (or lack thereof) to the reality of such an order, but it need not campaign against anyone's (even one's own) faith in the reality of such orders. What it does have to argue against is the theodicist assumption that morality, ethical seriousness, or having an ethical stance to the world necessarily presupposes there being a non- or superhuman ultimate order of meaningfulness.[5] Ethics, far from needing a larger context (e.g., a metaphysical or theological scheme of intelligibility) that makes it possible, is itself the fundamental (though non-foundational) context within which anything else, including any metaphysical account of the world in which suffering exists, is, or can be, articulated. Ethics, in Wittgenstein's (1974 [1921], §6.421) terms, is "transcendental."

The dispute between theodicies and antitheodicies is often seen as primarily, or even purely, metaphysical or, alternatively, almost exclusively ethical (as in "moral antitheodicies"). If the arguments of this book are on the

---

5 Even if that order is only partial and decentered in Aakko's (2025) sense.

right track, even partially, this dichotomy between the ethical and the metaphysical is itself part of the problem instead of being any solution to it. The project of antitheodicism highlights not the priority of ethics to metaphysics (or vice versa) but the deep, inextricable entanglement of the ethical and the metaphysical. What is at issue is our always already ethically concerned human way of viewing the world. Antitheodicism is grounded in the ethical affirmation of our fundamental need to recognize, both ontologically and ethically, individual sufferers' perspectives on reality in their distinctiveness and irreducibility. This entails rejecting theodicism as a pursuit of an overarching perspective of non-acknowledgment – a totalizing God's-Eye View. Furthermore, not only are the ethical and the metaphysical entangled here; similarly, the ethical and the conceptual critique of the confusions of theodicy are intertwined and inseparable (see Chapter 3). To be ethically confused is to be confused about one's world-engagement generally.

The question, then, is fundamentally about what morality is – about the nature of ethics as a human way of being in the world.[6] Even the questions of the philosophy of religion are, in the antitheodicist framework, subordinate to this issue. What, in the end, is morality? Why does it matter? How is our human ethical standing in the world structured? What is "the meaning of the ethical" for us (cf. again Gaita 2004 [1991])? These questions can, arguably, be only ethically and practically (or pragmatically) investigated, even though they may also be seen as transcendental questions in a quasi-Kantian sense, penetrating into the necessary conditions for the possibility of our living in a human world of meanings at all. The theodicist's and the antitheodicist's diverging conceptions of ethics are, it seems to me, *incommensurable* and can hardly argumentatively engage with each other without already presupposing their own basic points of departure.

There are, then, as already noted earlier, especially in Chapter 5, limits to how far an antitheodicist critique of theodicies and theodicism can argumentatively succeed. I would be tempted to say that turning from theodicism

---

6 In some of my earlier work on antitheodicy, I occasionally spoke of antitheodicism as a condition for the possibility of the moral (or ethical) point of view. Convinced by important critical remarks by my former student Panu-Matti Pöykkö (whose work on Levinas's antitheodicy is also a great source of inspiration for the present undertaking, as acknowledged earlier), I no longer use such phrases. Ethics is not a point of view we could adopt or fail to adopt; we are necessarily within ethics, prior to having any relation to the world around us at all. One way of formulating antitheodicism is to emphasize this self-sufficiency or overriding character of the ethical: any claim to ground the ethical in something else is already a (desperate, impossible, unthinkable) attempt to step outside the ethical sphere.

to antitheodicism amounts to a conversion, a new "lighting up" of an aspect, to continue to employ Wittgenstein-inspired expressions.[7] *Everything changes*, if we choose to view the world we live in in terms of antitheodicism instead of theodicism. This is also why I am inclined to associate antitheodicism with transcendental philosophy in the first place: like the Kantian transcendental conditions for the possibility of experience, it pertains to the constitutive conditions of our viewing the world (or anything) at all. Not a single element of our experienced world will remain unchanged after the "conversion" from theodicism to antitheodicism. It is important to understand the profundity of this change in one's ethical orientation in order to acknowledge the full significance of the antitheodicist challenge to the received views of theodicism.

When everything changes – when we view the entire world differently, taking seriously the (antitheodicist) recognition that there is a gap between the way the world is and the way it ought to be[8] – it is, however, crucial to consider what exactly this involves and what it doesn't. No one, I think, has expressed this better than Albert Camus, who concludes his "Letters to a German Friend" in 1944 as follows:

> The dawn about to break will mark your final defeat. I know that heaven, which was indifferent to your horrible victories, will be equally indifferent to your just defeat. Even now I expect nothing from heaven. But we shall at least have helped save man from the solitude to which you wanted to relegate him. (Camus 2020 [1945, 1960], 33.)

Taking the step toward an enhanced understanding of the ethical and the related revision of our entire relationship to the world we live in is not only significant for our personal moral development (our "soul-making," if you will, antitheodically conceived) but also for our lives as socially and politically engaged beings. In addition to emphasizing the infinite and absolute nature of our ethical duty to attend to others' suffering at the individual level, antitheodicism may remind us that we ought to learn to sincerely acknowledge others' suffering also in political contexts. Antitheodicism can never resolve the problem of evil and suffering for good, nor do much to alleviate

---

7 Consider, e.g., James's analysis of conversion in *The Varieties* (James 1958 [1902]), or Kuhn's (1970 [1962]) views on paradigm changes, also illustrated in terms of the duck-rabbit picture adopted from Wittgenstein (1953).
8 See Neiman's (2019) discussion of this essentially Kantian view in relation to the rejection of theodicies. In particular, note one important culmination of the criticism of theodicy in Nietzsche: we must "reevaluate all our values" when we give up traditional theodicy (ibid., 380). While not engaging with Nietzsche, something like this has, I suppose, been attempted by this book, too.

the real suffering that exists, but it can teach us how to construct, also in political contexts that can never fully avoid the consequentialism inherent in (secular) theodicies, stronger and more sensitive ethical arguments that could, on some rare occasions at least, even capture the conscience of our kings – if such a thing still exists.

REFERENCES

Aakko, Maikki. 2025. "Knowing Where We Are: On the Intelligibility of the World, Living Well and Meaningless Suffering". *International Journal of Philosophy and Theology* 85, 288–307.
Adams, Marilyn McCord. 1999. *Horrendous Evils and the Goodness of God*. Ithaca, NY and London: Cornell University Press.
Agamben, Giorgio. 2002 [1999]. *Remnants of Auschwitz: The Witness and the Archive*. Trans. D. Heller-Roazen. New York: Zone Books.
Alford, C. Fred. 2009. *After the Holocaust: The Book of Job, Primo Levi, and the Path to Affliction*. Cambridge: Cambridge University Press.
Appelqvist, Hanne, ed. 2020. *Wittgenstein and the Limits of Language*. London and New York: Routledge.
Arendt, Hannah. 1994 [1963]. *Eichmann in Jerusalem: A Report on the Banality of Evil*. London: Penguin.
Benatar, David. 2006. *Better Never to Have Been. The Harm of Coming into Existence*. Oxford: Oxford University Press.
Berckman, Edward M. 1976. "Brecht's Quarrel with God: From Anti-Theodicy to Eschatology". *Comparative Drama* 10, 130–146.
Bernstein, Richard. 2002. *Radical Evil: A Philosophical Interrogation*. Cambridge: Polity.
Bernstein, Richard. 2005. *The Abuse of Evil*. Cambridge: Polity.
Betenson, Toby. 2016. "Anti-theodicy". *Philosophy Compass* 11:1, 56–65.
Betenson, Toby. 2019. "Response to Lauri Snellman". *European Journal for Philosophy of Religion* 11:1, 213–226.
Bosman, Frank and van Wieringen, Archibald. 2021. "COVID-19 and the Secular Theodicy: On Social Distancing, the Death of God and the Book of Job". *The New Common*, March 20, 47–51.
Brachtendorff, Johannes. 2002. "Kants Theodizee-Aufsatz – Die Bedingungen des Gelingens philosophischen Theodizee". *Kant-Studien*. 93, 57–83.
Braiterman, Zachary. 1998. *(God) After Auschwitz: Tradition and Change in Post-Holocaust Jewish Thought*. Princeton, NJ: Princeton University Press.
Burley, Mikel. 2012a. *Contemplating Religious Forms of Life: Wittgenstein and D.Z. Phillips*. London and New York: Continuum/Bloomsbury.
Burley, Mikel. 2012b. "Contemplating Evil". *Nordic Wittgenstein Review* 1, www.nordicw ittgensteinreview.com.
Byrne, Peter. 2003. *God and Realism*. Aldershot: Ashgate.
Camus, Albert. 2020 [1945, 1960] "Letters to a German Friend". In Camus, *Committed Writings*. Trans. Justin O'Brien and Sandra Smith. London: Penguin, 1–33.

Card, Claudia. 2002. *The Atrocity Paradigm: A Theory of Evil*. New York: Oxford University Press.
Cavell, Stanley. 1979. *The Claim of Reason*. New York: Oxford University Press.
Chignell, Andrew P., ed. 2019a. *Evil: A History*. New York: Oxford University Press.
Chignell, Andrew P., ed. 2019b. "Evil, Unintelligibility, Radicality: Footnotes to a Correspondence Between Hannah Arendt and Karl Jaspers". In Andrew P. Chignell (ed.), *Evil: A History*. New York: Oxford University Press, 18–42.
Clement, W.D. 2020. "'The Excess of Glory Obscured': Behemoth and Anti-Theodicy in *Paradise Lost*". *Milton Quarterly* 54, 191–204.
Cole, Philip. 2006. *The Myth of Evil*. Edinburgh: Edinburgh University Press.
Cottingham, John. 2017. "Evil and the Meaning of Life". In Chad Meister and Paul K. Moser (eds.), *The Cambridge Companion to the Problem of Evil*. Cambridge: Cambridge University Press, 11–26.
Critchley, Simon. 2010. *Infinitely Demanding*. London: Verso.
Dahl, Espen. 2019. *The Problem of Job and the Problem of Evil*. Cambridge: Cambridge University Press.
Danielsson, Dennis Richard. 1982. *Milton's Good God: A Study in Literary Theodicy*. Cambridge: Cambridge University Press.
Davies, Paul. 2002. "Sincerity and the End of Theodicy: Three Remarks on Levinas and Kant". In Simon Critchley and Robert Bernasconi (eds.), *The Cambridge Companion to Levinas*. Cambridge: Cambridge University Press, 161–187.
Derrida, Jacques. 2004. "Capital Punishment: Another 'Temptation of Theodicy'". In Seyla Benhabib and Nancy Fraser (eds.), *Pragmatism, Critique, Judgment: Essays for Richard J. Bernstein*. Cambridge, MA and London: The MIT Press, 197–221.
Dostoevsky, Fedor. 2003. *The Brothers Karamazov*. Trans. David McDuff. London: Penguin.
Echazú, Gabriel. 2024a. "Does Moral Anti-theodicy Beg the Question?" *International Journal for Philosophy of Religion* 95, 115–130.
Echazú, Gabriel. 2024b. "Non-Ideal Theory in the Philosophy of Religion: Exploring Implications of Non-Ideal Theorising for the Problem of Evil". *Religious Studies* (early online), 1–16.
Fiala, Andrew. 2010. *Public War, Private Conscience: The Ethics of Political Violence*. London and New York: Continuum.
Fiala, Andrew. 2018. *Transformative Pacifism: Critical Theory and Social Practice*. London and New York: Bloomsbury.
Frankl, Viktor. 1988 [1969]. *The Will to Meaning: Foundations and Applications of Logotherapy*. New York: Plume.
Franklin, James. 2020. "Antitheodicy and the Grading of Theodicies by Moral Offensiveness". *Sophia* 59, 563–576.
Gaita, Raimond. 2000. *A Common Humanity: Thinking of Love and Truth and Justice*. London: Routledge.
Gaita, Raimond. 2004 [1991]. *Good and Evil: An Absolute Conception*. Rev. ed. London: Routledge.
Galbraith, Elizabeth C. 2006. "Kant and 'A Theodicy of Protest'". In Chris L. Firestone and Stephen R. Palmquist (eds.), *Kant and the New Philosophy of Religion*. Bloomington and Indianapolis: Indiana University Press, 179–189.
Garner, Daniel Osborn. 2012. *Antitheodicy, Atheodicy, and Jewish Mysticism in Post-Holocaust Theology: Atheodic Theologies after Auschwitz*. Piscataway, NJ: Gorgias Press.
Geddes, Jennifer L. 2018. "Theodicy, Useless Suffering, and Compassionate Asymmetry: Primo Levi, Emmanuel Levinas, and Anti-Theodicy". *Religions* 9, 114.

Gellman, Jerome, Meister, Chad, and Taliaferro, Charles, eds. 2018. *The History of Evil from the Mid-Twentieth Century to Today*. London: Routledge.
Gleeson, Andrew. 2012. *A Frightening Love: Recasting the Problem of Evil*. Basingstoke: Palgrave Macmillan.
Hick, John. 2010 [1966]. *Evil and the God of Love*. 3rd ed. Basingstoke: Palgrave Macmillan.
Hume, David. 1990 [1779]. *Dialogues Concerning Natural Religion*. London: Penguin.
Illman, Karl-Johan. 2003. "Theodicy in Job". In Antti Laato and Johannes C. de Moor (eds.), *Theodicy in the World of the Bible*. Leiden: Brill, 304–333.
van Inwagen, Peter. 2006. *The Problem of Evil*. Oxford: Clarendon Press.
James, William. 1979 [1897]. *The Will to Believe and Other Essays in Popular Philosophy*. Eds. Frederick H. Burkhardt, Fredson Bowers, and Ignas K. Skrupskelis. Cambridge, MA and London: Harvard University Press.
James, William. 1983 [1899]. *Talks to Teachers on Psychology and to Students on Some of Life's Ideals*. Eds. Frederick H. Burkhardt, Fredson Bowers, and Ignas K. Skrupskelis. Cambridge, MA and London: Harvard University Press.
James, William. 1958 [1902]. *The Varieties of Religious Experience*. New York: New American Library.
James, William. 1975 [1907]. *Pragmatism: A New Name for Some Old Ways of Thinking*. Eds. Frederick H. Burkhardt, Fredson Bowers, and Ignas K. Skrupskelis. Cambridge, MA and London: Harvard University Press.
Jankélévitch, Vladimir. 2005 [1967]. *Forgiveness*. Trans. Andrew Kelley. Chicago and London: The University of Chicago Press, 2013.
Jonas, Hans. 1996. *Mortality and Morality: A Search for the Good after Auschwitz*. Ed. Lawrence Vogel. Evanston, IL: Northwestern University Press.
Judt, Tony. 1992. *Past Imperfect: French Intellectuals 1944 – 1956*. Berkeley: University of California Press.
Kant, Immanuel. 1983. *Immanuel Kant: Werke in zehn Bänden*. Ed. Wilhelm Weischedel. Darmstadt: Wissenschaftliche Buchgesellschaft (Contains, e.g., "Über das Misslingen aller philosophischen Versuche in der Theodicee", vol. 9.)
Kant, Immanuel. 1990 [1781/1787]. *Kritik der reinen Vernunft*. Ed. Raymund Schmidt. Hamburg: Felix Meiner.
Kant, Immanuel. 2018 [1793–94]. *Religion within the Boundaries of Mere Reason*. Ed. and trans. Allen Wood and George Di Giovanni. Cambridge: Cambridge University Press (Contains, in addition to *Religion*, "On the Miscarriage of All Philosophical Trials in Theodicy" [1791], 17–36.)
Keltz, Kyle B., ed. 2025. *The Palgrave Handbook on the Problem of Animal Suffering in the Philosophy of Religion*. Cham: Palgrave Macmillan.
Kivistö, Sari and Pihlström, Sami. 2016. *Kantian Antitheodicy: Philosophical and Literary Varieties*. Basingstoke: Palgrave Macmillan.
Kivistö, Sari and Pihlström, Sami. 2017. "Theodicies as Failures of Recognition". *Religions* 8, 242.
Koistinen, Timo. 2011. "D.Z. Phillips' Contemplative Conception of Philosophy". *Neue Zeitschrift für systematische Theologie und Religionsphilosophie* 53, 333–356.
Koistinen, Timo. 2022. "A Wittgensteinian Antitheodicy". *Religions* 13, 1113.
Kuhn, Thomas S. 1970 [1962]. *The Structure of Scientific Revolutions*. 2nd ed. Chicago and London: University of Chicago Press.
Laato, Antti and de Moor, Johannes C., eds. 2003. *Theodicy in the World of the Bible* Leiden: Brill.

Leibniz, Gottfried Wilhelm. 1985 [1710]. *Essais de théodicée sur la bonté de Dieu, la liberté de l'homme et l'origine du mal / Die Theodizee von der Güte Gottes, der Freiheit des Menschen und dem Ursprung des Übels*. In Leibniz, *Philosophische Schriften*, vol. 2. Ed. Herbert Herring. Darmstadt: Wissenschaftliche Buchgesellschaft.

Levi, Primo. 1996 [1958]. *Survival in Auschwitz: The Nazi Assault on Humanity*. Trans. Stuart Woolf. New York: Touchstone Books (Also known with the title, *If This Is a Man*.)

Levi, Primo. 1988 [1986]. *The Drowned and the Saved*. Trans. Raymond Rosenthal. London: Michael Joseph.

Levinas, Emmanuel. 1987 [1974]. *Otherwise than Being or beyond Essence*. Trans. Alphonso Lingis. Pittsburgh, PA: Duquesne University Press.

Levinas, Emmanuel. 2006 [1982]. "Useless Suffering". In Levinas, *Entre-nous: Thinking-of-the-other*. Trans. Michael B. Smith and Barbara Harshav. London: Continuum, 78–87.

Little, Daniel. 2022. *Confronting Evil in History*. Cambridge: Cambridge University Press.

van der Lugt, Mara. 2021. *Dark Matters: Pessimism and the Problem of Suffering*. Princeton, NJ: Princeton University Press.

van der Lugt, Mara. 2025. *Hopeful Pessimism*. Princeton, NJ: Princeton University Press.

Mackie, J.L. 1955. "Evil and Omnipotence". *Mind* 64, 200–212.

Martin, Michael J. 1990. *Atheism. A Philosophical Justification*. Philadelphia: Temple University Press.

Mavelli, Luca. 2016. "Governing Uncertainty in a Secular Age: Rationalities of Violence, Theodicy and Torture". *Security Dialogue* 47, 117–132.

McLaughlin, Ryan P. 2025a. "Dissonant Theodicy: Theodicy and Anti-Theodicy in Irresolvable Tension". In B. Kyle Keltz (ed.), *The Palgrave Handbook on the Problem of Animal Suffering in the Philosophy of Religion*. Cham: Palgrave Macmillan, 129–169.

McLaughlin, Ryan P. 2025b. "Theodicy, Anti-Theodicy, and Ethics: Some Considerations". In Keltz (ed.), *The Palgrave Handbook on the Problem of Animal Suffering in the Philosophy of Religion*. Cham: Palgrave Macmillan, 521–550.

McMahan, Jeff. 2009. *Killing in War*. Oxford: Clarendon Press.

Meister, Chad and Moser, Paul K., eds. 2017. *The Cambridge Companion to the Problem of Evil*. Cambridge: Cambridge University Press.

Montanye, James A. 2024. "Democracy as Secular Theodicy". *Journal of Libertarian Studies* 28:1, jls.mises.org.

Morgan, David and Wilkinson, Iain. 2001. "The Problem of Suffering and the Sociological Task of Theodicy". *European Journal of Social Theory* 4, 199–214.

Mulhall, Stephen. 1994. *Faith and Reason*. London: Duckworth.

Murdoch, Iris. 2007 [1971]. *The Sovereignty of Good*. London: Penguin.

Nagasawa, Yujin. 2024. *The Problem of Evil for Atheists*. Oxford: Oxford University Press.

Namli, Elena. 2022. "*The Brothers Karamazov* and the Theology of Suffering". *Studies in East European Thought* 74, 19–36.

Neiman, Susan. 2002. *Evil in Modern Thought: An Alternative History of Philosophy*. Princeton, NJ: Princeton University Press.

Neiman, Susan. 2019. "What Happened to Evil?" In Andrew P. Chignell (ed.), *Evil: A History*. New York: Oxford University Press, 358–382.

Newsom, Carol A. 2019. "Evil in the Hebrew Bible: The Case of the Wisdom Literature". In Andrew P. Chignell (ed.), *Evil: A History*. New York: Oxford University Press, 60–81.

Noddings, Nel. 2018. "Education and Approaches to Evil". In Victoria S. Harrison (ed.), *The History of Evil in the Early Twentieth Century*. London and New York: Routledge, 26–42.

Phillips, D.Z. 1977. "The Problem of Evil" and "Postscript". In Stuart C. Brown (ed.), *Reason and Religion*. Ithaca, NY and London: Cornell University Press, 103–121, 135–139.
Phillips, D.Z. 1991. *From Fantasy to Faith*. Basingstoke: Palgrave.
Phillips, D.Z. 1993. *Wittgenstein and Religion*. Basingstoke and New York: Palgrave.
Phillips, D.Z. 2004. *The Problem of Evil and the Problem of God*. London: SCM.
Phillips, D.Z. 2005. "The Holocaust and Language". In John K. Roth (ed.), *Genocide and Human Rights: A Philosophical Guide* Basingstoke: Palgrave Macmillan, 46–64.
Pihlström, Sami. 2011. *Transcendental Guilt: Reflections on Ethical Finitude*. Lanham, MD: Lexington.
Pihlström, Sami. 2013. *Pragmatic Pluralism and the Problem of God*. New York: Fordham University Press.
Pihlström, Sami. 2014. *Taking Evil Seriously*. Basingstoke: Palgrave Macmillan.
Pihlström, Sami. 2017. "Why There Should Be No Argument *from* Evil: Remarks on Recognition, Antitheodicy, and Impossible Forgiveness". *International Journal of Philosophy and Theology* 77, 523–538.
Pihlström, Sami. 2019. "A Pragmatist Approach to the Mutual Recognition between Ethico-Political and Theological Discourses on Evil and Suffering". *Political Theology* 20, 157–175.
Pihlström, Sami. 2020a. *Pragmatic Realism, Religious Truth, and Antitheodicy: On Viewing the World by Acknowledging the Other*. Helsinki: Helsinki University Press.
Pihlström, Sami. 2020b. "Theodicy by Other Means? Rethinking 'God after Auschwitz' through the Dialectics of Antitheodicism". *Cosmos and History* 16, 474–493. Reprinted in Pihlström 2021, chapter 6.
Pihlström, Sami. 2021. *Pragmatist Truth in the Post-Truth Age: Sincerity, Normativity, and Humanism*. Cambridge: Cambridge University Press.
Pihlström, Sami. 2022. *Toward a Pragmatist Philosophy of the Humanities*. Albany: SUNY Press.
Pihlström, Sami. 2023. *Humanism, Antitheodicism, and the Critique of Meaning in Pragmatist Philosophy of Religion*. Lanham, MD: Lexington.
Pihlström, Sami, ed. 2024. *The Bloomsbury Handbook of Pragmatism*. London and New York: Bloomsbury.
Pihlström, Sami. 2025. *"The Unthinkable" in Ethics, History, and Philosophical Anthropology: A Pragmatic-Transcendental View*. London and New York: Bloomsbury.
Pihlström, Sami. 2026. "Secular Theodicies – a Transcendental-Pragmatist Critique". Forthcoming in Lauri Snellman and Francis Jonbäck (eds.), *Theodicies and Antitheodicies*. Cham: Springer.
Pihlström, Sami and Kivistö, Sari. 2023. *Critical Distance: Ethical and Literary Engagements in Detachment, Isolation, and Otherness*. Cham: SpringerBriefs.
Pinnock, Sarah K. 2002. *Beyond Theodicy: Jewish and Christian Continental Thinkers Respond to the Holocaust*. Albany: SUNY Press.
Plantinga, Alvin. 1977. *God, Freedom, and Evil*. Grand Rapids, MI: Eerdmans.
Plantinga, Alvin. 2000. *Warranted Christian Belief*. Oxford Oxford University Press.
Posti, Mikko. 2019. *Divine Providence in Medieval Philosophical Theology 1250–1350*. Leuven: Peeters.
Pöykkö, Panu-Matti. 2023. *The Ambivalent Other: A Transcendental Reading of Emmanuel Levinas*. Diss. Helsinki: University of Helsinki.

Rakhmanin, Aleksei. 2024. "Albert Camus's Political Antitheodicy". In Panu-Matti Pöykkö, Pamela Slotte, and Viljami Salo (eds.), *Political Violence: Historical, Philosophical, and Theological Perspectives*. Berlin: de Gruyter, 209–227.

Roth, John K. 2001. "A Theodicy of Protest". In Stephen T. Davis (ed.), *Encountering Evil: Live Options in Theodicy*. Louisville, KY: Westminster John Knox Press, 1–37.

Roth, John K. 2004. "Theistic Antitheodicy". *American Journal of Theology and Philosophy* 25, 276–293.

Rowe, William, ed. 2001. *God and the Problem of Evil*. Malden, MA and Oxford: Blackwell.

Saarinen, Risto. 2019. "Gifts and Burdens: Elaborating Pihlström's Antitheodicy". In Henrik Rydenfelt, Heikki J. Koskinen, and Mats Bergman (eds.), *Limits of Pragmatism and Challenges of Theodicy: Essays in Honour of Sami Pihlström*. Acta Philosophica Fennica 95. Helsinki: The Philosophical Society of Finland, 143–152.

Sachs, Carl B. 2011. "The Acknowledgment of Transcendence: Anti-theodicy in Adorno and Levinas". *Philosophy and Social Criticism* 37, 273–294.

Sarot, Marcel. 2003. "Theodicy and Modernity: An Inquiry into the Historicity of Theodicy". In Antti Laato and Johannes C. de Moor (eds.), *Theodicy in the World of the Bible*. Leiden: Brill, 1–26.

Scarry, Elaine. 1987. *The Body in Pain: The Making and Unmaking of the World*. Oxford: Oxford University Press.

Schopenhauer, Arthur. 1969 [1819, 1844]. *The World as Will and Representation*, 2 vols. Trans. E.F.J. Payne. New York: Dover.

Scott, Mark S. M. 2015. *Pathways in Theodicy: An Introduction to the Problem of Evil*. Philadelphia, PA: Augsburg Fortress Press.

Schönbaumsfeld, Genia. 2018. "On the Very Idea of a Theodicy". In Mikel Burley (ed.), *Wittgenstein, Religion and Ethics: New Perspectives from Philosophy and Theology*. London and New York: Bloomsbury, 93–112.

Schönbaumsfeld, Genia. 2021. "Was ist eigentlich eine Theodizee?" In Oliver Wiertz (ed.), *Logische Brillianz – Ruchlose Denkungsart? Möglichkeiten und Grenzen der Diskussion des Problems des Übels in der analytischen Religionsphilosophie*. Münster: Aschendorff, 105–124.

Shearn, Samuel. 2013. "Moral Critique and Defence of Theodicy". *Religious Studies* 49, 439–458.

Shook, John R. 2016. "What the Hell Is God Up To? God's Evils and the Theodicies Holding God Responsible". In Benjamin W. McCraw and Robert Arp (eds.), *The Problem of Evil: New Philosophical Directions*. Lanham, MD: Lexington, 127–140.

Simpson, Robert Mark. 2009. "Moral Antitheodicy: Prospects and Problems". *International Journal for Philosophy of Religion* 65, 153–169.

Snellman, Lauri. 2019. "'Anti-theodicy' and Antitheodicies". *European Journal for Philosophy of Religion* 11:1, 201–211.

Snellman, Lauri. 2023. *Evil and Intelligibility: A Grammatical Metacritique of the Problem of Evil*. Leiden: Brill.

Sollereder, Bethany N. 2019. *God, Evolution, and Animal Suffering: Theodicy without a Fall*. London and New York: Routledge.

Sontag, Susan. 2003. *Regarding the Pain of Others*. London: Penguin.

Sterba, James, ed. 2017. *Ethics and the Problem of Evil*. Bloomington and Indianapolis: Indiana University Press.

von Stosch, Klaus. 2013. *Theodizee*. Paderborn: Schöningh.

Stump, Eleonore. 2010. *Wandering in Darkness: Narrative and the Problem of Suffering*. Oxford: Clarendon Press.

Surin, Kenneth. 1986. *Theology and the Problem of Evil*. Oxford: Blackwell.
Swinburne, Richard. 1977. "The Problem of Evil". In Stuart C. Brown (ed.), *Reason and Religion*. Ithaca, NY and London: Cornell University Press, 81–102.
Swinburne, Richard. 1998. *Providence and the Problem of Evil*. Oxford: Oxford University Press.
Särkelä, Arvi. 2025. "'The Truly Apocalyptic View': Physiognomy of a Critical Gesture in Wittgenstein". Forthcoming in *Critical Times* 8:3 (Paper presented at the University of Helsinki, March 24, 2025).
Tilghman, Benjamin R. 1994. *An Introduction to the Philosophy of Religion*. Oxford: Blackwell.
Tilley, Terrence W. 1991. *The Evils of Theodicy*. Washington, DC: Georgetown University Press.
Trakakis, N.N. 2013. "Antitheodicy". In J.P. McBrayer and D. Howard-Snyder (eds.), *The Blackwell Companion to the Problem of Evil*. Malden, MA: Blackwell-Wiley, 363–376.
Trakakis, N.N. 2017. "Anti-Theodicy". In Chad Meister and Paul K. Moser (eds.), *The Cambridge Companion to the Problem of Evil*. Cambridge: Cambridge University Press, 124–143.
Trakakis, N.N. 2018. "Anti-theodicy". In Jerome Gellman, Chad Meister, and Charles Taliaferro (eds.), *The History of Evil from the Mid-Twentieth Century to Today*. London: Routledge, 137–151.
Trakakis, N.N., ed. 2018. *The Problem of Evil: Eight Views in Dialogue*. Oxford: Oxford University Press.
Trakakis, N.N. 2021. "'And Therefore I Hasten to Return My Ticket': Anti-theodicy Radicalised". *Sophia* 60, 799–620.
Trakakis, N.N. 2023. *Idealism after Existentialism: Encounters in Philosophy of Religion*. London and New York: Routledge.
Udoff, Alan, ed. 2013. *Vladimir Jankélévitch and the Question of Forgiveness*. Lanham, MD: Lexington.
Walzer, Michael. 1992 [1977]. *Just and Unjust Wars: A Moral Argument with Historical Illustrations*. 2nd ed. New York: Basic Books.
Weber, Max. 1956 [1922]. *The Sociology of Religion*. Trans. Ephraim Fischoff. Boston: Beacon Press.
West, Cornel. 1989. *The American Evasion of Philosophy: A Genealogy of Pragmatism*. Madison and London: University of Wisconsin Press.
Wiertz, Oliver J., ed. 2021a. *Logische Brillianz – Ruchlose Denkungsart? Möglichkeiten und Grenzen der Diskussion des Problems des Übels in der analytischen Religionsphilosophie*. Münster: Aschendorff.
Wiertz, Oliver J. 2021b. "Das Problem des Übels in der analytischen Religionsphilosophie: Geschichtliche Stationen und Kritik". In Oliver J. Wiertz (ed.), *Logische Brillianz – Ruchlose Denkungsart? Möglichkeiten und Grenzen der Diskussion des Problems des Übels in der analytischen Religionsphilosophie*. Münster: Aschendorff, 29–104.
Williams, Bernard. 2006. "Unbearable Suffering". In Williams, *The Sense of the Past: Essays in the History of Philosophy*. Ed. Miles Burnyeat. Princeton, NJ: Princeton University Press, 331–340.
Wittgenstein, Ludwig. 1974 [1921]. *Tractatus Logico-Philosophicus*. Trans. David F. McGuinness and David F. Pears. London: Routledge and Kegan Paul.
Wittgenstein, Ludwig. 1958 [1953]. *Philosophical Investigations*. Trans. G.E.M. Anscombe. Oxford: Blackwell.

Wittgenstein, Ludwig, 1961. *Notebooks 1914–1916*. Eds. G.E.M. Anscombe and G.H. von Wright. Oxford: Blackwell.
Wittgenstein, Ludwig. 1998 [1980]. *Culture and Value*. Eds. G.H. von Wright and Heikki Nyman, rev. ed. Alois Pichler. Oxford: Blackwell.
Wood, Allen. 2020. *Kant and Religion*. Cambridge: Cambridge University Press.

INDEX

Note: Words such as "theodicy", "theodicism", "antitheodicy", "antitheodicism", "evil", and "suffering" occur throughout the book on most pages and are therefore not indexed, unless specified (e.g., "Kantian antitheodicy").

Aakko, Maikki 116
Adams, Marilyn McCord 25, 35
Alford, C. Fred 93
animal suffering 82
anthropocentrism 81
anthropomorphism 81
antinatalism 96–97
Arendt, Hannah 16, 56, 60
Augustine 5, 25, 71
authentic theodicy 37

banality of evil, the 16, 60
Bayle, Pierre 31–32, 97
Benatar, David 96–97
Bernstein, Richard 9, 16, 33, 55–56, 85
Betenson, Toby 49
Book of Job 3, 8, 35–36, 52, 65, 93
Braiterman, Zachary 8, 31, 101
Burley, Mikel 49
Byrne, Peter 27–28

Camus, Albert 67, 120
Christianity 32, 102
communism 67
conceptual *vs.* moral antitheodicy 18, 83
counterpurposiveness 33–34
Covid–19 13, 61, 63–65, 67
critical distance 99
critique of meaning 29

Dewey, John 20, 41, 68
disproportionality 52
Dostoevsky, Fedor 56, 100–103

Echazú, Gabriel 107–8
Enlightenment, the 37
evidentialism *vs.* fideism 24, 26

forgiveness 57–58
Frankl, Viktor 68, 109–10
Franklin, James 78–80
free will theodicy 4

Gaita, Raimond 10, 45, 51, 72–73, 82, 105–6, 112–13
Gaza 61
Geddes, Jennifer L. 94
Gleeson, Andrew 45, 47
God 1, 3–5, 17, 22, 27, 31–35, 46, 48–50, 54, 57, 59, 61, 65–66, 79–81, 85–86, 94–95, 99–101, 111
God's–Eye–View, the 15, 27, 61, 78, 110, 119
Grotius, Hugo 71

harmony 87–88, 102
health–care ethics 63
Hegelian theodicy 42, 86
historiography 89–91
Holocaust, the 1, 14, 19, 48, 51–58, 65, 68, 89, 92, 105–7, 110
Holocaust denialism 106
humanism 78–82
Hume, David 3, 23, 31

immeasurability (of suffering) 15
instrumentalization (of suffering) 2, 6, 13–14, 29
van Inwagen, Peter 25, 35
Irenaeus 25

James, William 9, 20, 38, 40–44, 56, 60–61, 68, 84, 86
Jankélévitch, Vladimir 57

Jewish (post–Holocaust) antitheodicism 55–56
Jonas, Hans 54–55, 66, 84
Judt, Tony 67
just war theory, the 69–75, 115
justification 50

Kant, Immanuel 8, 31–42, 47, 52, 59–60, 71, 78, 85, 99, 109, 115
Kantian antitheodicy 38–41
Karamazov, Ivan (fictional character) 56–57, 65, 100–103, 116

Leibniz, Gottfried Wilhelm 3–5, 39, 79
Leibnizian ("best possible world") theodicy 4, 41–42, 65, 79, 86
Levi, Primo 92–95, 105, 109, 112
Levinas, Emmanuel 9, 16, 51–55, 84–85, 87, 105, 115
Levinasian antitheodicy 51–58
logical *vs.* evidential problem of evil and suffering 22
van der Lugt, Mara 7–8, 29, 31–32, 37, 40, 77, 81, 96

Mackie, J.L. 23
Malcolm, Norman 45
Malebranche, Nicolas 31
Mavelli, Luca 68–69
McMahan, Jeff 71
meaningfulness *vs.* meaninglessness 21, 28, 46, 74, 89–91, 95, 108–13, 116
meaning-making 29, 37, 68, 99, 110–13, 115
meliorism (*vs.* optimism and pessimism) 8, 21, 29, 40, 43–44, 60–61, 77, 90–91, 96–98, 112
meliorist antitheodicy 96
Merleau-Ponty, Maurice 67
metaphysical realism 27
metaphysics 38
Milton, John 47
morality 116–17
Mulhall, Stephen 46–47
Murdoch, Iris 112

Nagasawa, Yujin 5
Namli, Elena 103
NATO 69–70
naturalism 61
Nazis/Nazism 71–73, 75, 93
Neiman, Susan 37, 116, 120

normative status of theodicism *vs.* antitheodicism 24
nuclear weapons 74

optimism 28, 39, 41–42, 60–61, 97–98
Orwell, George 108

pacifism 71–72, 75, 115
Peirce, Charles S. 20, 40
pessimism 28–29, 39, 42–43, 97–98
Phillips, D.Z. 9, 45, 47–51, 84
Plantinga, Alvin 25, 35
postulates of practical reason 85; *see also* Kant, I.
pragmatism 6, 20–21, 59–64, 68, 83–84, 86
pragmatist antitheodicy/antitheodicism 40–44, 63
prayer 93–94
price 15, 64
providence 92–95, 110

radical evil 33, 85; *see also* Kant, I.
realism *vs.* antirealism 26–27, 61, 90–91
Rhees, Rush 45
Rousseau, Jean-Jacques 31

Särkelä, Arvi 112
Sartre, Jean-Paul 67
Schopenhauer, Arthur 8, 31, 38–41
secular theodicy/theodicism 6, 8, 59–76, 115
securitization 68
Shearn, Samuel 100
Simpson, Mark 79, 107
sincerity 36, 98
skeptical theism 22
Snellman, Lauri 18, 116
soul 45, 89
soul-making theodicy 4, 26, 49
Stump, Eleonore 116
Suarez, Francisco 71
supreme emergency 73–74
Swinburne, Richard 35, 47–48

teleology 66
theism *vs.* atheism 21–23, 117–18
theodicist logic 5, 40
theodicy *vs.* mere defense 4, 22, 25
Thomas Aquinas 71
torture 69
Trakakis, N.N. 17, 31, 101–3
transcendental antitheodicism 9–10, 19–20, 53, 98–109

INDEX 133

transcendental arguments/argumentation 6, 111
transcendental illusion 37
transcendental philosophy 42
transcendental *vs.* transcendent 99
trolley problem 80, 82
truth 44
truthfulness 36

Ukraine, Russian invasion of 61, 69–71
unthinkable, the 10, 62, 74–75, 98–109, 115, 117
utilitarianism 14, 40

Voltaire 31

Walzer, Michael 71–74
Wiertz, Oliver J. 100
Wilde, Oscar 49
Winch, Peter 45
Wittgenstein, Ludwig 45, 87, 112, 118
Wittgensteinian antitheodicy/antitheodicism 45–51, 87
Wittgensteinian moral philosophy 9

www.ingramcontent.com/pod-product-compliance
Lightning Source LLC
Chambersburg PA
CBHW032028230426
43671CB00005B/240